150
BAKING
recipes
INSPIRED IDEAS FOR EVERYDAY COOKING

150
CAKE
recipes

150
CHICKEN
recipes

150
CUPCAKE & MUFFIN
recipes
INSPIRED IDEAS FOR EVERYDAY COOKING

150
FAST & SIMPLE
recipes
INSPIRED IDEAS

150
INDIAN
recipes
INSPIRED IDEAS FOR EVERYDAY COOKING

150
PASTA
recipes
INSPIRED IDEAS FOR EVERYDAY COOKING

150
SLOW COOKER
recipes
INSPIRED IDEAS FOR EVERYDAY COOKING

150
STIR-FRY
recipes
INSPIRED IDEAS FOR EVERYDAY COOKING

150
STUDENT
recipes
INSPIRED IDEAS FOR EVERYDAY COOKING

150
TAPAS
recipes
INSPIRED IDEAS FOR EVERYDAY COOKING

150
VEGETARIAN
recipes
INSPIRED IDEAS FOR EVERYDAY COOKING

150

FAST
& SIMPLE
recipes

....

INSPIRED IDEAS FOR
EVERYDAY COOKING

CONTENTS

INTRODUCTION

Our busy and bustling lifestyles mean that many of us have limited time to spend in the kitchen preparing and cooking a meal, especially during the week. As a result, sometimes we may just reach for a quick snack instead of eating a full meal, or select a ready-meal for speed and convenience.

But things are about to change and this book will ensure that mealtimes are no longer a case of grab-and-eat. Every tempting recipe in this book can be prepared and cooked within 45 minutes from start to finish, and some will take even less time. You'll be impressed and surprised at the vast array of delicious dishes you can rustle up in that length of time, resulting in a multitude of marvellous meals to suit a hectic lifestyle, many of which are sure to earn a regular slot at your table. These hassle-free dishes don't lack in flavour either and the range of recipes will appeal to adults, children and teenagers alike – there really is something for everyone! Also included are a few practical time-saving tips to keep you on course for speedy success in the kitchen.

The first chapter starts with a delectable selection of light bites, including a choice of soups, salads, dips and sliders, as well as patties, fritters, fajitas and wontons. Choose from savoury delights like Quick Tomato Soup, Smoked Mackerel Salad and Baked Chicken Wings, or delve into some more exotic dishes, such as Falafel Patties, Pork Spring Rolls and Crab Wontons.

Some magnificent meat and poultry dishes are featured in the next chapter, many of which are ideal for sharing. Fantastic family favourites include the impressive Speedy Roast Chicken, Quick Spaghetti Bolognese, Ham & Leek Risotto and Pork & Apple One Pot, while other dishes such as Lamb and Feta Burgers, Parma Ham and Red Pepper Pizza and Pork Pad Thai are perfect for enjoying with friends.

The next chapter encompasses terrific fish and seafood dishes, including Peppered Tuna Steaks, Smoked Salmon Tagliatelle and Spicy Thai Seafood Stew, as well as some ever-popular classics such as brilliant Baked 'Fish and Chips', Moules Marinières and Speedy Paella.

For vegetarians or those who want to cut down on their meat and fish intake, a comprehensive collection of fast and fabulous vegetarian dishes make up the next chapter with food from all over the globe. Take inspiration from Speedy Vegetable Lasagne, Celeriac, Chestnut, Spinach & Feta Filo Pies, Risotto with Peas and Gorgonzola, or Aubergine Gratin.

Finally, to satisfy those with a sweet tooth, a sensational selection of desserts and bakes form the final scrumptious chapter. Choose from delightful desserts such as Summer Berry Tarts, Apple Fritters, Quick Tiramisù, Mini Apple Crumbles and Lemon Posset. Or, if you fancy a snack on the move or a quick break at any time of the day, many of these recipes will provide the perfect sweet treat, including Fruity Flapjacks, Blueberry Scones, Chewy Golden Cookies and Lemon Drizzle Squares.

Time-saving Tips

* Be organized and plan your meals for the week ahead

* Go food shopping with a list of everything you need and don't be tempted to stray from your list – this will save you both time and money

* When you are ready to get cooking, read through the recipe and gather all the equipment together that you need. Preheat the oven if required

* Gather and weigh out all your ingredients and prepare them before you begin. Now you are ready to get cooking and creative in the kitchen!

INTRODUCTION

LIGHT BITES

QUICK TOMATO SOUP	8
SPICY CHICKEN NOODLE SOUP	10
MEDITERRANEAN FISH SOUP	12
SMOKED MACKEREL SALAD	14
TOMATO, OLIVE & MOZZARELLA PASTA SALAD	16
GREEK SALAD	18
ROAST CHICKEN SALAD WITH ORANGE DRESSING	19
GUACAMOLE DIP	20
EGG TORTILLA WITH FETA & SWEETCORN	22
BAKED MUSHROOMS WITH HERBED RICOTTA	24
FALAFEL PATTIES	26
CHICKEN SLIDERS	28
CHICKEN & HERB FRITTERS	29
BAKED CHICKEN WINGS	30
CHICKEN NUGGETS WITH BARBECUE SAUCE	31
MEATBALL SANDWICH	32
WARM SLICED BEEF TABBOULEH SALAD	34
PAPRIKA STEAK WRAPS WITH HORSERADISH CREAM	36
PORK SPRING ROLLS	38
CHIPOTLE PORK FAJITAS	40
CHILLI LAMB CUTLETS	42
FISH TACOS WITH AVOCADO SALSA	44
COD FISH CAKES	46
BAKED SCALLOPS	47
CALAMARES	48
PRAWN COCKTAIL WITH QUAIL EGGS	50
CRAB WONTONS	52
SEAFOOD TEMPURA	54

QUICK TOMATO SOUP

Serves: 4 **Prep: 10 mins** **Cook: 10–15 mins**

Ingredients

2 tbsp olive oil

1 large onion, chopped

400 g/14 oz canned whole plum tomatoes

300 ml/10 fl oz vegetable stock

1 tbsp tomato purée

1 tsp hot pepper sauce

handful of fresh basil leaves

salt and pepper

Method

1 Heat the oil in a large saucepan over a medium heat, then add the onion and fry for 4–5 minutes, stirring, until soft. Add the tomatoes, stock, tomato purée, hot pepper sauce and half the basil leaves.

2 Process using a hand-held blender until smooth. Stir the soup over a medium heat until just boiling, then season to taste with salt and pepper.

3 Serve in warmed serving bowls, garnished with the remaining basil leaves.

★ Variation

For a smoky twist on this classic soup, replace the canned tomatoes with roasted red peppers. Oil some whole red peppers and roast under a hot grill, turning frequently, until the skin is blackened. Remove the charred skin, stalks and seeds, and roughly chop.

SPICY CHICKEN NOODLE SOUP

Serves: 2　　　　**Prep: 15 mins**　　　　**Cook: 10-15 mins**

Ingredients

300 ml/10 fl oz chicken stock

1 x 18 g/¾ oz sachet miso paste

2-cm/¾-inch piece fresh ginger, peeled and finely grated

1 red chilli, deseeded and thinly sliced

1 carrot, peeled and cut into thin strips

200 g/7 oz pak choi, roughly chopped

150 g/5½ oz dried egg thread noodles, cooked

1 cooked chicken breast, shredded

dark soy sauce, to taste

4 spring onions, trimmed and finely chopped

handful fresh coriander, roughly chopped, to serve

Method

1　Place the stock and 250 ml/9 fl oz boiling water in a saucepan and bring to boil over a medium–high heat. Add the miso paste and simmer for 1–2 minutes.

2　Add the ginger, chilli, carrot, pak choi, cooked noodles and chicken. Simmer for a further 4–5 minutes. Season to taste with soy sauce.

3　Scatter the spring onions in the base of two warmed serving dishes and pour the soup over. Top with chopped coriander and serve immediately.

MEDITERRANEAN FISH SOUP

Serves: 4   **Prep: 15 mins**   **Cook: 15 mins**

Ingredients

1 tbsp olive oil

1 large onion, chopped

2 garlic cloves, finely chopped

425 ml/15 fl oz fish stock

150 ml/5 fl oz dry white wine

1 bay leaf

1 sprig each fresh thyme, rosemary and oregano

450 g/1 lb firm white fish fillets (such as cod, monkfish or halibut), skinned and cut into 2.5-cm/1-inch cubes

450 g/1 lb fresh mussels, prepared

400 g/14 oz canned chopped tomatoes

225 g/8 oz fresh prawns, peeled and deveined

salt and pepper

fresh thyme sprigs, to garnish

fresh bread, to serve

Method

1 Heat the olive oil in a large saucepan and gently fry the onion and garlic for 2–3 minutes, or until just softened.

2 Pour in the stock and wine, and bring to the boil. Tie the bay leaf and herbs together with clean string and add to the saucepan together with the fish. Discard any mussels with broken shells or any that refuse to close when tapped. Add to the saucepan and stir well, cover and simmer for 5 minutes.

3 Stir in the tomatoes and prawns, and continue to cook for a further 3–4 minutes, or until piping hot, the fish is cooked through and the prawns have turned pink.

4 Discard the herbs and any mussels that remain closed. Season to taste, then ladle into warmed bowls. Garnish with sprigs of fresh thyme and serve with fresh bread.

SMOKED MACKEREL SALAD

Serves: 4   **Prep: 15–20 mins**   **Cook: 15 mins**

Ingredients

4 eggs

175 g/6 oz broccoli, cut into small florets

300 g/10½ oz smoked mackerel fillet, skinned

1 crisp eating apple, such as Gala

crusty bread, to serve

Dressing

juice of 1 lemon, plus extra for sprinkling

2 tbsp extra light mayonnaise

1 tsp Dijon mustard

2 tbsp snipped fresh chives

salt and pepper

Method

1 Place the eggs in a saucepan of cold water. Bring the pan to the boil over a high heat and boil for 10 minutes. Drain the eggs, crack the shells and rinse in cold water. Peel and cut into slices.

2 Meanwhile, bring a saucepan of water to the boil over a high heat. Place the broccoli in the pan and boil for 3–4 minutes. Drain and rinse in cold water.

3 Slice the mackerel diagonally into strips. Core and slice the apple, sprinkling with a little lemon juice.

4 To make the dressing, place the lemon juice, mayonnaise, mustard and chives in a jar and shake well to mix evenly. Season to taste with salt and pepper.

5 Combine the eggs, broccoli, mackerel and apple in a salad bowl and pour in the dressing, tossing with two forks to mix thoroughly, then serve immediately with crusty bread.

TOMATO, OLIVE & MOZZARELLA PASTA SALAD

Serves: 4 **Prep: 15–20 mins, plus cooling** **Cook: 15 mins**

Ingredients

225 g/8 oz dried conchiglie

50 g/1¾ oz pine nuts

350 g/12 oz cherry tomatoes, halved

1 red pepper, deseeded and cut into bite-size chunks

1 red onion, chopped

200 g/7 oz mozzarella, cut into small pieces

12 black olives, stoned

25 g/1 oz fresh basil leaves

fresh Parmesan cheese shavings, to garnish

salt

Dressing

5 tbsp extra virgin olive oil

2 tbsp balsamic vinegar

1 tbsp chopped fresh basil

salt and pepper

Method

1 Bring a large saucepan of lightly salted water to the boil. Add the pasta, bring back to the boil and cook for 8–10 minutes, until tender but still firm to the bite. Drain, refresh under cold running water and drain again. Leave to cool.

2 Meanwhile, heat a dry frying pan over a low heat, add the pine nuts and cook, shaking the pan frequently, for 1–2 minutes, until lightly toasted. Remove from the heat, transfer to a dish and leave to cool.

3 To make the dressing, put all the ingredients in a small bowl and mix together well. Cover with clingfilm and set aside.

4 Divide the pasta between serving bowls. Add the pine nuts, tomatoes, pepper, onion, mozzarella and olives to each bowl. Sprinkle over the basil, then drizzle over the dressing. Garnish with Parmesan cheese shavings and serve immediately.

GREEK SALAD

Serves: 4   **Prep: 15 mins**   **Cook: No cooking**

Ingredients

6–8 vine leaves

4 tomatoes, sliced

½ cucumber, peeled and sliced

1 small red onion, sliced thinly

115 g/4 oz feta cheese, cubed

8 black olives

Dressing

3 tbsp extra virgin olive oil

1 tbsp lemon juice

½ tsp dried oregano

salt and pepper

Method

1 To make the dressing, blend together all the ingredients in a small bowl, or put into a screw-top jar and shake until well blended.

2 Arrange the vine leaves on a serving dish and then the tomatoes, cucumber and onion. Scatter the cheese and olives on top. Pour the dressing over the salad, season and serve immediately.

LIGHT BITES

ROAST CHICKEN SALAD WITH ORANGE DRESSING

Serves: 4   **Prep: 20–25 mins**   **Cook: No cooking**

Ingredients

250 g/9 oz spinach leaves

handful of fresh flat-leaf parsley, plus extra sprigs to garnish

1½ cucumbers, thinly sliced

90 g/3¼ oz walnuts, toasted and chopped

350 g/12 oz boneless lean roast chicken, thinly sliced

2 red apples

1 tbsp lemon juice

Dressing

2 tbsp extra virgin olive oil

juice of 1 orange

finely grated rind of ½ orange

1 tbsp soured cream

Method

1 Wash and drain the spinach and parsley leaves, reserving a few sprigs of parsley to garnish. Arrange on a large serving platter and top with the cucumber and some of the walnuts. Arrange the chicken slices on top of the leaves.

2 Core the apples, then cut them in half. Cut each half into slices and brush with the lemon juice to prevent discoloration. Arrange the apple slices over the salad.

3 To make the dressing, blend together all the ingredients in a small bowl, or put into a screw-top jar and shake until well blended. Drizzle the dressing over the salad, garnish with the reserved parsley sprigs and remaining walnuts, and serve immediately.

LIGHT BITES

GUACAMOLE DIP

Serves: 4   **Prep: 15 mins**   **Cook: No cooking**

Ingredients

2 large avocados

juice of 1–2 limes

2 large garlic cloves, crushed

1 tsp mild chilli powder, or to taste, plus extra to garnish

salt and pepper

breadsticks, to serve

Method

1 Cut the avocados in half. Remove the stones and skin, and reserve the flesh.

2 Place the avocado flesh in a food processor with the juice of one or two limes, according to taste. Add the garlic and chilli powder and process until smooth.

3 Season to taste with salt and pepper. Transfer to a serving bowl, garnish with chilli powder and serve with breadsticks for dipping.

EGG TORTILLA WITH FETA & SWEETCORN

Serves: 4　　　　**Prep: 15 mins**　　　　**Cook: 20 mins**

Ingredients

350 g/12 oz potatoes, cubed

2 tbsp olive oil

1 onion, chopped

1 courgette, coarsely grated

200 g/7 oz canned sweetcorn, drained

6 eggs

100 g/3½ oz feta cheese, crumbled

salt and pepper

paprika, to garnish

Method

1 Cook the potatoes in a saucepan of lightly salted boiling water for 5 minutes, or until just tender. Drain well.

2 Heat the oil in a large ovenproof frying pan over a medium heat. Add the onion and cook for 5 minutes, stirring occasionally, until softened. Add the courgette and potatoes, and cook for 2 minutes. Stir in the sweetcorn.

3 Preheat the grill to high. Place the eggs in a bowl. Season to taste with salt and pepper and lightly whisk together. Pour over the vegetables, then sprinkle over the feta cheese and leave to cook for 4–5 minutes, until almost set.

4 Cook under the preheated grill for 2–3 minutes, until bubbling and golden brown. Transfer to a wooden board or warmed serving plates. Garnish with paprika and serve hot or cold.

BAKED MUSHROOMS WITH HERBED RICOTTA

Serves: 4　　　　**Prep: 15 mins**　　　　**Cook: 15–20 mins**

Ingredients

4 large, flat mushrooms
1 tbsp olive oil
1 shallot, roughly chopped
25 g/1 oz fresh flat-leaf parsley
1 tbsp snipped fresh chives
140 g/5 oz ricotta cheese
salt and pepper

Method

1 Preheat the oven to 200°C/400°F/Gas Mark 6. Remove the stalks from the mushrooms and set aside. Place the mushrooms in a shallow baking dish and brush with the oil.

2 Put the mushroom stalks, shallot, parsley and chives in a food processor and process until finely chopped. Season to taste with salt and pepper.

3 Place the chopped ingredients in a large bowl with the ricotta and stir to mix evenly.

4 Spoon the herbed ricotta onto the top of the mushrooms. Bake in the preheated oven for 15–20 minutes, or until tender and bubbling. Serve immediately.

FALAFEL PATTIES

Serves: 4   **Prep: 15–20 mins**   **Cook: 5 mins**

Ingredients

800 g/1 lb 12 oz canned chickpeas, drained and rinsed

1 small onion, chopped

zest and juice of 1 lime

2 tsp ground coriander

2 tsp ground cumin

plain flour, for dusting

4 tbsp olive oil

fresh basil sprigs, to garnish

tomato salsa, to serve

Method

1 Place the chickpeas, onion, lime zest and juice, and the spices into a food processor or blender and process to a coarse paste. Transfer the mixture to a large mixing bowl.

2 Divide the mixture into eight balls, dust with flour, then flatten slightly to make a patty shape of your preferred thickness.

3 Heat the oil in a large frying pan over a medium heat. Add the patties and cook for 2 minutes. Turn the burgers and cook for a further 2 minutes, until cooked through and crisp.

4 Transfer to warmed serving plates. Garnish with basil sprigs and serve with tomato salsa.

CHICKEN SLIDERS

Makes: 4

Prep: 15–20 mins

Cook: 8 mins,
plus optional toasting

Ingredients

4 chicken breast fillets
(about 1-cm/½-inch thick)

225 ml/8 fl oz buttermilk

125 g/4½ oz plain flour

1 tbsp sweet paprika or
smoked paprika

2 tsp garlic powder

1 tsp pepper

1 tsp salt

½ tsp cayenne pepper

125 ml/4 fl oz vegetable oil

4 hamburger buns

1 large tomato

4 tbsp mayonnaise

4 lettuce leaves

450 g/1 lb prepared
coleslaw, to serve

Method

1 Place the chicken breasts in a bowl with the buttermilk and toss to coat.

2 Put the flour into a shallow bowl and add the paprika, garlic powder, pepper, salt and cayenne pepper. Stir to mix. Remove the chicken fillets, one at a time, from the buttermilk and dip them in the flour mixture. Return to the buttermilk and dip again in the flour mixture. Heat the oil in a large frying pan over a medium–high heat until very hot. Add the fillets in a single layer and cook for about 3 minutes on each side, until golden brown and cooked through.

3 Split the buns and toast them if desired. Slice the tomato. Spread mayonnaise on the top half of each bun. Place a tomato slice and a lettuce leaf on the base of each bun. Top with a chicken fillet. Serve immediately with coleslaw on the side.

LIGHT BITES

CHICKEN & HERB FRITTERS

Serves: 4　　　　　**Prep: 20 mins**　　　**Cook: 5–10 mins**

Ingredients

500 g/1 lb 2 oz mashed potato

250 g/9 oz cooked chicken, chopped

125 g/4½ oz cooked ham, finely chopped

1 tbsp fresh mixed herbs

2 eggs, lightly beaten

1 tbsp milk

125 g/4½ oz fresh wholemeal breadcrumbs

oil, for shallow-frying

salt and pepper

mixed salad leaves, to serve

Method

1 Place the potato, chicken, ham, herbs and one of the eggs in a large mixing bowl. Season to taste with salt and pepper, and mix together.

2 Divide the mixture into small portions and shape each into a ball.

3 Beat the remaining egg with the milk in a wide, shallow dish. Place the breadcrumbs in a separate wide, shallow dish.

4 Coat the chicken balls in the egg mixture, allowing any excess to drip back into the dish, then coat in the breadcrumbs.

5 Heat the oil in a large frying pan over a medium heat and cook the fritters until they are golden brown.

6 Transfer to a warmed serving dish and serve immediately with mixed salad leaves.

LIGHT BITES

BAKED CHICKEN WINGS

Serves: 4   **Prep: 15–20 mins**   **Cook: 22–23 mins**

Ingredients

12 chicken wings
1 egg
4 tbsp milk
70 g/2½ oz plain flour
1 tsp paprika
225 g/8 oz breadcrumbs
55 g/2 oz butter
salt and pepper

Method

1 Preheat the oven to 220°C/425°F/Gas Mark 7. Separate each chicken wing into three pieces, discarding the bony tip. Beat the egg with the milk in a shallow dish.

2 Combine the flour, paprika, and salt and pepper to taste in a shallow dish. Place the breadcrumbs in another dish. Dip the chicken in the egg mixture, drain and roll in the flour.

3 Shake off any excess, then roll the chicken wings in the breadcrumbs, gently pressing them onto the surface and shaking off any excess.

4 Put the butter in a wide, shallow roasting tin and place in the preheated oven to melt. Place the chicken in the tin skin-side down.

5 Bake for 10 minutes on each side. To check the wings are cooked through, cut into the middle and ensure there are no remaining traces of pink or red. Any juices that run out should be clear and piping hot with visible steam rising.

6 To serve, transfer the chicken to a warmed serving platter.

LIGHT BITES

CHICKEN NUGGETS WITH BARBECUE SAUCE

Serves: 4   **Prep: 15 mins**   **Cook: 15 mins**

Ingredients

4 tbsp dry breadcrumbs

2 tbsp grated Parmesan cheese

2 tsp chopped fresh thyme,

2 boneless chicken breasts

115 g/4 oz melted butter

salt and pepper

Barbecue sauce

55 g/2 oz butter

2 large onions, grated

300 ml/10 fl oz cider vinegar

300 ml/10 fl oz tomato ketchup

175 g/6 oz dark brown sugar

1–2 tsp Worcestershire sauce

salt and pepper

Method

1 Preheat the oven to 200°C/400°F/Gas Mark 6. Place the breadcrumbs, cheese and thyme in a wide, shallow bowl. Season to taste with salt and pepper, and mix together.

2 Remove any skin from the chicken and cut into cubes. Coat the pieces in the melted butter, allowing any excess to drip back into the dish, then coat in the crumb mixture.

3 Arrange the chicken pieces in a single layer on a large baking sheet. Bake in the preheated oven for 10 minutes, until the chicken is cooked through.

4 Meanwhile, to make the sauce, heat the butter in a large saucepan over a low heat. Add the onions and cook until soft, but not brown. Add the cider vinegar, tomato ketchup, sugar and Worcestershire sauce. Season to taste with salt and pepper and heat, stirring, until the sugar has completely dissolved. Bring to the boil then reduce the heat and simmer for 5 minutes.

5 Transfer the chicken to a warmed serving dish and serve immediately with the sauce.

LIGHT BITES

MEATBALL SANDWICH

Serves: 4　　　**Prep: 15–20 mins**　　　**Cook: 21–25 mins**

Ingredients

400 g/14 oz lean beef mince

1 onion, grated

1 garlic clove, crushed

2 tsp mild chilli powder

25 g/1 oz fresh wholemeal breadcrumbs

oil, for shallow-frying

salt and pepper

To serve

lettuce leaves

4 sub rolls, halved lengthways

1 red onion, thinly sliced into rings

Method

1 Place the mince in a large mixing bowl. Add the onion, garlic, chilli powder and breadcrumbs. Season to taste with salt and pepper, and mix together. Use a small ice-cream scoop to shape the mixture into small balls.

2 Heat a shallow depth of oil in a deep frying pan until very hot. Add the meatballs in batches and fry for 8–10 minutes, until cooked through.

3 Lift out the meatballs with a slotted spoon and drain on absorbent kitchen paper.

4 Place the lettuce leaves on the bottom halves of the rolls and top with the meatballs. Place the onion rings on top, cover with the lids and serve immediately.

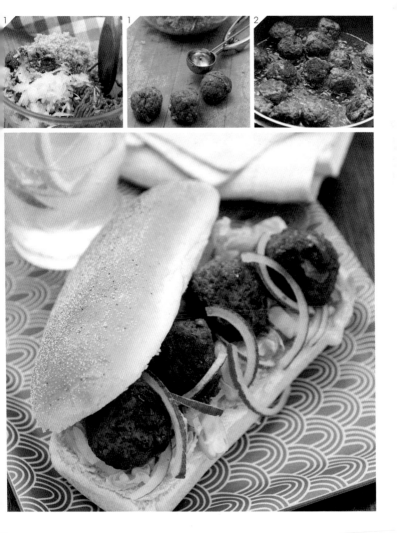

WARM SLICED BEEF TABBOULEH SALAD

Serves: 4   **Prep: 15–20 mins**   **Cook: 10 mins, plus standing**

Ingredients

100 g/3½ oz bulgar wheat
400 g/14 oz lean beef fillet
200 g/7 oz fresh flat-leaf parsley, finely chopped
140 g/5 oz fresh mint, finely chopped
1 red onion, thinly sliced
2 tomatoes, diced
1 tbsp extra virgin olive oil, plus extra for brushing
juice of 2 lemons
salt and pepper

Method

1 Place the bulgar wheat in a bowl and pour over boiling water to cover. Leave to soak for 10 minutes. Drain thoroughly, pressing out any excess moisture.

2 Meanwhile, place a griddle pan or frying pan over a high heat. Season the beef fillet with salt and pepper, brush lightly with oil and cook for 2–3 minutes on each side, turning once. Remove from the heat and cover with foil for 5 minutes.

3 Mix together the parsley, mint, onion, tomatoes and bulgar wheat in a bowl. Stir in the olive oil and lemon juice, and season to taste with salt and pepper.

4 Slice the beef fillet into 2.5-cm/1-inch thick strips. Serve the bulgar wheat salad on a large serving platter and arrange the beef slices on top, then pour over the meat juices.

PAPRIKA STEAK WRAPS WITH HORSERADISH CREAM

Serves: 4　　　　**Prep: 15–20 mins**　　　　**Cook: 10 mins, plus resting**

Ingredients

4 sirloin steaks, about 175 g/6 oz each

1 garlic clove, crushed

2 tsp smoked paprika, plus extra for sprinkling

sunflower oil, for brushing

100 g/3½ oz crème fraîche

3 tbsp creamed horseradish

8 small flour tortillas

75 g/2¾ oz rocket

2 ripe avocados, peeled, stoned and sliced

1 red onion, thinly sliced

salt and pepper

Method

1 Spread the steaks with the garlic and sprinkle both sides with the paprika. Season to taste with salt and pepper.

2 Preheat a ridged griddle pan over a very high heat and brush with oil. Add the steaks and cook for 6–8 minutes, turning once. Remove from the heat and leave to rest for 5 minutes.

3 Meanwhile, place the crème fraîche and horseradish in a small bowl and mix together. Using half the horseradish cream, spread a thin layer over each tortilla.

4 Slice the steaks into strips. Divide between the tortillas with the rocket, avocado and red onion, wrapping the sides over. Serve immediately with an extra spoonful of horseradish cream, sprinkled with a little more paprika.

PORK SPRING ROLLS

Makes: 20

Prep: 20 mins,
plus soaking & cooling

Cook: 25 mins

Ingredients

6 dried Chinese mushrooms, soaked in warm water for 20 minutes

1 tbsp vegetable or groundnut oil, plus extra for deep-frying

225 g/8 oz minced pork

1 tsp dark soy sauce

100 g/3½ oz canned bamboo shoots, rinsed and julienned

pinch of salt

100 g/3½ oz raw prawns, peeled, deveined and chopped

225 g/8 oz beansprouts, trimmed and roughly chopped

1 tbsp finely chopped spring onions

20 spring roll wrappers

1 egg white, lightly beaten

Method

1 Squeeze out any excess water from the mushrooms and finely slice, discarding any tough stems.

2 Heat a wok or large, heavy-based saucepan over a high heat, then add the oil. Add the pork and stir-fry until it is cooked through and no longer pink.

3 Add the dark soy sauce, bamboo shoots, mushrooms and the salt. Stir over a high heat for 3 minutes.

4 Add the prawns and cook for 2 minutes, until they turn pink. Add the beansprouts and cook for a further minute. Remove from the heat and stir in the spring onions. Leave to cool.

5 Place a tablespoon of the mixture towards the bottom of a spring roll wrapper. Roll once to secure the filling, then fold in the sides to create a 10-cm/4-inch piece and continue to roll up. Seal with egg white.

6 Heat enough oil for deep-frying in a large wok or large, heavy-based saucepan to 180–190°C/350–375°F, or until a cube of bread browns in 30 seconds. Fry the rolls for about 5 minutes, until golden brown and crispy.

CHIPOTLE PORK FAJITAS

Serves: 4 **Prep: 20 mins** **Cook: 20–23 mins**

Ingredients

8–12 flour tortillas
1 tbsp ground chipotle chilli
2 tsp soft light brown sugar
1 tsp salt
1 tsp ground cumin
1 tsp dried oregano
½ tsp garlic powder
1 pork fillet
2 bacon rashers
1 onion
1 red pepper
1 orange or yellow pepper
1 tbsp olive oil
1 tbsp garlic purée

To serve

salsa
chopped avocado
soured cream
2 limes, halved
fresh mint leaves, to garnish

Method

1 Preheat the oven to 200°C/400°F/Gas Mark 6, wrap the tortillas in foil and place in the oven to warm. Combine the ground chilli, sugar, salt, cumin, oregano and garlic powder in a small bowl.

2 Slice the pork into 5-mm/¼-inch thick rounds, then cut the rounds into 1-cm/½-inch wide strips. Dice the bacon. Put the pork and bacon into a large bowl with the spice mixture and toss. Slice the onion, red pepper and orange pepper into 1-cm/½-inch wide strips.

3 Heat the oil in a large frying pan over a medium–high heat. Add the pork and bacon and cook, stirring, for 4–5 minutes, until the meat is brown. Transfer to a plate. Add the onion, garlic purée, red pepper and orange pepper to the pan, and cook for about 4 minutes, until the vegetables begin to soften. Return the meat to the pan and fry until cooked through.

4 Serve immediately with the warmed tortillas, salsa, avocado, soured cream and limes. Garnish with fresh mint leaves.

CHILLI LAMB CUTLETS

Serves: 4　　　　**Prep: 15 mins**　　　　**Cook: 14–17 mins,**
plus resting

Ingredients

60 g/2¼ oz fresh flat-leaf parsley

2 garlic cloves

juice of 1 lemon

1–2 red or green chillies

1 tbsp sweet paprika

4 tbsp olive oil

4 x 5-cm/2-inch thick lamb cutlets

salt and pepper

pittas, to serve

Salad

1 cucumber

1 tbsp fresh flat-leaf parsley

225 g/8 oz cherry tomatoes

juice of 1 lemon

½ tsp salt

Method

1 Put the parsley, garlic, lemon juice, chillies, paprika and 1 teaspoon of salt into a food processor and process until smooth. Add the oil and process to combine. Season the lamb with salt and pepper, then coat on both sides with some of the sauce. Reserve the remaining sauce.

2 To make the salad, dice the cucumber, finely chop the parsley and halve the tomatoes, then put them all into a medium-sized bowl. Toss with the lemon juice and salt, and set aside until ready to serve.

3 Heat a ridged griddle pan over a medium–high heat. Add the chops and cook for about 6 minutes on each side for medium-rare, or a bit longer for medium. Remove from the heat and leave to rest for a few minutes before serving. Meanwhile, warm the bread under the grill. Serve the chops with the bread, salad and reserved sauce.

FISH TACOS WITH AVOCADO SALSA

Serves: 4   **Prep: 20 mins**   **Cook: 10-15 mins**

Ingredients

Salsa

½ red onion, diced

2 jalapeño peppers, deseeded and diced

2 tomatoes, diced

½ avocado, diced

2 tbsp chopped fresh coriander

3 tbsp lime juice

½ tsp salt

Fish

2 tbsp lime juice

1 tbsp olive oil

1 tsp ground cumin

1 tsp chilli powder

½ tsp salt

400 g/14 oz white fish fillets

To serve

8 small corn tortillas (25 g/1 oz each)

300 g/10½ oz red cabbage, shredded

Method

1 Put all the salsa ingredients in a mixing bowl and stir to mix well.

2 Preheat a grill to medium–high or put a griddle pan over a medium–high heat. In a small bowl, combine the lime juice, olive oil, cumin, chilli powder and salt.

3 Brush the lime mixture on both sides of the fish fillets. Grill the fish over a medium–high heat for 2–4 minutes per side, or until grill marks start to appear and the fish is opaque and cooked through. Chop the fish into bite-sized chunks.

4 To serve, warm the tortillas under the grill, then top them with the fish, salsa and shredded cabbage. Serve immediately with extra salsa on the side.

COD FISH CAKES

Serves: 4 **Prep: 15–20 mins** **Cook: 17–20 mins**

Ingredients

450 g/1 lb skinless cod fillet

450 g/1 lb mashed potato

4 spring onions, finely chopped

2 tbsp chopped parsley

1 small egg, beaten

plain flour, for shaping

sunflower oil, for shallow-frying

salt and pepper

green vegetables and lemon wedges, to serve

Method

1 Place the cod in a wide saucepan and add just enough boiling water to cover. Bring to the boil, then reduce the heat, cover and simmer for 4–5 minutes, until the fish flakes easily. Drain very thoroughly.

2 Place the fish in a large mixing bowl. Add the mashed potatoes, onions, parsley and egg. Season to taste with salt and pepper, and mix together.

3 Divide the mixture into eight portions and shape each into a ball. Then, on a floured surface, flatten slightly to make a patty shape of your preferred thickness.

4 Heat a shallow depth of oil in a large frying pan until very hot. Add the fish cakes and cook for 6–8 minutes, turning once, until golden brown. Drain on kitchen paper.

5 Transfer to warmed serving plates and serve immediately with green vegetables and lemon wedges.

LIGHT BITES

BAKED SCALLOPS

Serves: 4 **Prep: 15 mins** **Cook: 15–20 mins**

Ingredients

700 g/1 lb 9 oz shelled scallops, chopped, shells reserved

2 onions, finely chopped

2 garlic cloves, finely chopped

3 tbsp chopped fresh parsley

pinch of freshly grated nutmeg

pinch of ground cloves

2 tbsp fresh white breadcrumbs

2 tbsp olive oil

salt and pepper

Method

1 Preheat the oven to 200°C/400°F/Gas Mark 6. Mix together the scallops, onions, garlic, 2 tablespoons of the parsley, the nutmeg and cloves in a bowl, and season to taste with salt and pepper.

2 Divide the mixture between four scrubbed scallop shells or heatproof dishes. Sprinkle the breadcrumbs and remaining parsley on top and drizzle with the olive oil.

3 Bake the scallops in the preheated oven for 15–20 minutes, or until lightly golden and piping hot. Serve immediately.

LIGHT BITES

CALAMARES

Serves: 6

Prep: 15–20 mins   **Cook: 18–22 mins**

Ingredients

450 g/1 lb squid, prepared, cleaned and cut into rings

plain flour, for coating

sunflower oil, for deep-frying

salt

lemon wedges, to garnish

garlic mayonnaise, to serve

Method

1 Slice the squid into 1-cm/½-inch rings and halve the tentacles if large. Rinse under cold running water and dry well with kitchen paper. Dust the squid rings with flour so that they are lightly coated.

2 Preheat the oven to low. Heat enough oil for deep-frying in a large, heavy-based saucepan to 180–190°C/350–375°F, or until a cube of bread browns in 30 seconds. Fry the squid rings in small batches, for 2–3 minutes, or until golden brown and crisp all over, turning several times. Do not overcrowd the pan.

3 Remove with a slotted spoon and drain well on kitchen paper. Keep warm in the preheated oven while you fry the remaining squid rings.

4 Sprinkle the fried squid rings with salt and serve immediately, garnished with lemon wedges and with garlic mayonnaise for dipping.

PRAWN COCKTAIL WITH QUAIL EGGS

Serves: 4   **Prep: 20 mins**   **Cook: 10 mins**

Ingredients

8 quail eggs

6 tbsp mayonnaise

3 tbsp Greek-style yogurt

2 tbsp tomato ketchup

dash of Tabasco sauce

2 tsp lime juice

40 g/1½ oz peppery salad leaves

5-cm/2-inch piece of cucumber, finely diced

1 small, ripe avocado, peeled and thinly sliced

225 g/8 oz cooked king prawns, peeled and tails left intact

salt and pepper

lime wedges and fresh dill sprigs, to garnish

Method

1 Bring a small saucepan of water to the boil then reduce to a simmer. Gently lower the quail eggs into the water and simmer for 5 minutes. Drain and cool under cold running water. Once cold, peel and set aside.

2 Place the mayonnaise, yogurt, ketchup, Tabasco and lime juice in a bowl, and mix together thoroughly. Season to taste with salt and pepper.

3 Divide the salad leaves between four large wine or cocktail glasses. Scatter over the diced cucumber. Halve the eggs and arrange on top of the salad with the avocado slices and prawns (reserving eight prawns to garnish).

4 Spoon over the mayonnaise dressing. Serve garnished with the reserved prawns, lime wedges and sprigs of dill.

CRAB WONTONS

Makes: 20

Prep: 20 mins,
plus cooling

Cook: 17 mins

Ingredients

1 tbsp groundnut or vegetable oil, plus extra for deep-frying

2.5-cm/1-inch piece fresh ginger, peeled and finely chopped

¼ red pepper, deseeded and finely chopped

handful of fresh coriander, chopped

¼ tsp salt

150 g/5½ oz canned white crabmeat, drained

20 wonton wrappers

water, for brushing

sweet chilli dipping sauce, to serve

Method

1 Heat a wok over a high heat, then add the oil. Add the ginger and red pepper, and stir-fry for 30 seconds.

2 Add the coriander and mix well. Leave to cool, then add the salt and the crabmeat, and mix again. Meanwhile, remove the wonton wrappers from the packet, but keep in a pile covered with clingfilm to prevent them from drying out.

3 Lay one wrapper on a work surface in front of you and brush the edges with water. Put a teaspoonful of the crabmeat mixture in the centre and fold the wrapper over the mixture to form a triangle.

4 Press the edges together to seal. Fold each side corner up to the top corner to make a small parcel, brushing the edges with water to seal, if necessary. Repeat with the remaining wrappers and crabmeat mixture.

5 Heat enough oil for deep-frying in a large wok to 180–190°C/350–375°F, or until a cube of bread browns in 30 seconds. Add the wontons, in batches, and cook for 45 seconds–1 minute, until crisp and golden all over. Remove with a slotted spoon, drain on kitchen paper and keep warm while you cook the remaining wontons. Serve warm with sweet chilli dipping sauce.

SEAFOOD TEMPURA

Serves: 6   **Prep: 15 mins**   **Cook: 25–30 mins**

Ingredients

8 large, raw prawns, peeled and deveined

150 g/5½ oz packet tempura mix

8 squid rings, prepared and cleaned

4 live scallops, shucked and cleaned

200 g/7 oz firm white fish fillets, cut into strips

vegetable oil, for deep-frying

few drops sesame oil

shoyu (Japanese soy sauce), to serve

Method

1 Make little cuts on the underside of the prawns to keep them straight while they cook.

2 Prepare the tempura mix according to the packet instructions in a large bowl until you have a lumpy batter full of air bubbles. Do not try to make the batter smooth or it will be heavy, and use it straight away or it will settle. Drop all the seafood and fish into the batter.

3 Heat the vegetable oil in a large, heavy-based saucepan to 180–190°C/350–375°F, or until a cube of bread browns in 30 seconds. Add the sesame oil.

4 Deep-fry 5–6 tempura pieces at a time, for 2–3 minutes, until they turn a very light golden colour. Do not overcrowd the pan. Remove and drain on kitchen paper for 30 seconds. Serve hot with shoyu as a dipping sauce.

★ **Variation**

This light, crispy batter is perfect for making vegetable tempura too. Slice some sweet potato and courgette, then dip in the batter and fry. Serve garnished with lots of fresh herbs and lemon.

MEAT & POULTRY

SPEEDY ROAST CHICKEN

Serves: 4   **Prep: 20 mins**   **Cook: 23–25 mins**

Ingredients

2 tbsp olive oil, plus extra if needed

1 small onion, chopped

450 g/1 lb Brussels sprouts

450 g/1 lb small, red-skinned new potatoes

12 baby carrots

1 fennel bulb

4 skinned chicken legs (thighs and drumsticks)

4 tbsp Dijon mustard

4 tbsp clear honey

1 tbsp white wine vinegar

2 tsp garlic purée

¼–½ tsp cayenne pepper

50 ml/2 fl oz chicken stock or water

1 tbsp fresh oregano leaves

50 ml/2 fl oz dry white wine

salt and pepper

Method

1 Preheat the oven to 240°C/475°F/Gas Mark 9. Heat the oil in a large, ovenproof frying pan. Stir the onion into the pan. Trim and quarter the sprouts. Add them to the pan and stir. Quarter the potatoes and add them to the pan. Peel the carrots but leave them whole. Add them to the pan. Trim, quarter and core the fennel, then slice it into small wedges and add to the pan.

2 Generously season the chicken with salt and pepper. Push the vegetables to the side of the pan. If necessary, add a little more oil to the pan. Add the chicken to the pan and cook for 2–3 minutes, until brown on one side, then turn. Meanwhile, combine the mustard, honey, vinegar, garlic purée, 1 teaspoon salt, cayenne pepper and stock in a bowl. Spoon over the turned chicken pieces to coat well. Drizzle the remaining sauce over the vegetables. Scatter the oregano over the chicken and vegetables.

3 Transfer the pan to the preheated oven and cook for about 20 minutes, until the vegetables are cooked, the chicken is tender and the juices run clear when a skewer is inserted into

the thickest part of the meat. Remove the pan from the oven and pour in the wine, stirring the vegetables up a bit and deglazing the pan. Serve immediately on warmed plates.

★ Variation

To give this dish a Spanish twist, replace the Brussels sprouts, potatoes and carrots with sliced red peppers, peas and thick slices of chorizo. Add a little smoked paprika instead of the Dijon mustard to give it an authentic Spanish flavour.

CHICKEN WITH CREAMY PENNE

Serves: 2   **Prep: 10 mins**   **Cook: 16–19 mins**

Ingredients

200 g/7 oz dried penne

1 tbsp olive oil

2 skinless, boneless chicken breasts

4 tbsp dry white wine

115 g/4 oz frozen peas

5 tbsp double cream

salt

4–5 tbsp chopped fresh parsley, to garnish

Method

1 Bring a large saucepan of lightly salted water to the boil. Add the pasta, bring back to the boil and cook for about 8–10 minutes, until tender but still firm to the bite. Drain.

2 Meanwhile, heat the oil in a frying pan over a medium heat. Add the chicken breasts and cook, turning once, for 8–10 minutes, until the chicken is tender and the juices run clear when a skewer is inserted into the thickest part of the meat.

3 Pour in the wine and cook over a high heat until it has almost evaporated.

4 Add the peas, cream and pasta to the frying pan and stir well. Cover and simmer for 2 minutes.

5 Transfer to warmed serving plates. Garnish with fresh parsley and serve immediately.

MOZZARELLA-STUFFED CHICKEN BREASTS

Serves: 4   **Prep: 15–20 mins**   **Cook: 15–20 mins**

Ingredients

4 skinless chicken breast fillets

4 tsp green pesto

125 g/4½ oz mozzarella cheese

4 thin slices Parma ham

250 g/9 oz cherry plum tomatoes, halved

75 ml/2½ fl oz dry white wine or chicken stock

1 tbsp olive oil

salt and pepper

fresh ciabatta, to serve

Method

1 Preheat the oven to 220°C/425°F/Gas Mark 7. Place the chicken breasts on a board and cut a deep pocket into each with a sharp knife. Place a teaspoonful of pesto in each pocket.

2 Cut the cheese into four equal pieces and divide between the chicken breasts, tucking into the pockets.

3 Wrap a slice of ham around each chicken breast to enclose the filling, with the join underneath. Place the chicken in a shallow ovenproof dish and arrange the tomatoes around it. Season with salt and pepper, pour over the wine and drizzle with the oil.

4 Bake in the preheated oven for 15–20 minutes, until the chicken is tender and the juices run clear when a skewer is inserted into the thickest part of the meat.

5 Cut the chicken breasts in half diagonally, place on warmed serving plates with the tomatoes and spoon over the juices. Serve with fresh ciabatta.

CHICKEN & DUMPLINGS

Serves: 4　　　　**Prep: 10 mins**　　　　**Cook: 25–35 mins**

Ingredients

2 tbsp olive oil

1 large onion

2 celery sticks

2 carrots

1 tbsp fresh thyme leaves

1 tsp salt

½ tsp pepper

4 tbsp butter

60 g/2¼ oz plain flour

2 tbsp milk

1.4 litres/2½ pints chicken stock

1 rotisserie chicken

140 g/5 oz frozen peas

2 tbsp fresh parsley leaves, to garnish

Dumplings

2 tbsp butter

30 g/1 oz fresh chives

250 g/9 oz plain flour

2 tsp baking powder

¾ tsp salt

225 ml/8 fl oz milk

Method

1 Heat the oil in a large, heavy-based saucepan over a medium–high heat. Dice the onion, celery and carrots, and add them to the pan. Cook, stirring, for about 3 minutes until the onion is translucent. Add the thyme, salt and pepper, and cook for a further minute. Add the butter and heat until melted, then stir the flour into the butter. Cook until the butter and flour have browned. Stir in the milk and add the stock. Bring to the boil, then reduce the heat to medium and simmer for about 10 minutes. Meanwhile, pull the meat from the chicken carcass and shred it.

2 To make the dumplings, place the butter in a microwave-safe dish. Cover the dish and heat in the microwave on a low setting for 30 seconds, or until melted. Finely chop the chives. Put the flour, baking powder and salt into a bowl and stir to combine. Stir in the butter, milk and chives until just combined.

3 Stir the chicken and peas into the vegetables, then drop small spoonfuls of the dumpling batter on top. Cover and simmer for 12–15 minutes, until the dumplings are cooked through. Meanwhile, finely chop the parsley. Ladle the casserole and dumplings into bowls. Garnish with parsley and serve immediately.

MEAT & POULTRY

CAJUN CHICKEN GUMBO

Serves: 2   **Prep: 15 mins**   **Cook: 25 mins**

Ingredients

1 tbsp sunflower oil

4 chicken thighs

1 small onion, diced

2 celery sticks, diced

1 small green pepper, deseeded and diced

85 g/3 oz long-grain rice

300 ml/10 fl oz chicken stock

1 fresh red chilli, thinly sliced

250 g/9 oz okra

1 tbsp tomato purée

salt and pepper

Method

1 Heat the oil in a large frying pan over a medium heat. Add the chicken and cook until golden. Remove the chicken from the pan using a slotted spoon. Add the onion, celery and green pepper to the pan and cook for 1 minute. Pour off any excess fat.

2 Add the rice and cook, stirring briskly, for a further minute. Add the chicken stock and bring to the boil.

3 Add the chilli and okra to the pan with the tomato purée. Season to taste with salt and pepper.

4 Return the chicken to the pan and stir. Cover tightly and simmer gently for 15 minutes, until all the liquid has been absorbed, the chicken is tender and the juices run clear when a skewer is inserted into the thickest part of the meat. Stir occasionally and, if the mixture becomes too dry, add a little extra stock. Transfer to warmed serving plates and serve immediately.

CHICKEN BREASTS WITH PARMESAN CRUMB TOPPING

Serves: 4   **Prep: 15 mins**   **Cook: 20 mins**

Ingredients

4 skinless, boneless chicken breasts

5 tbsp pesto sauce

40 g/1½ oz ciabatta breadcrumbs

25 g/1 oz Parmesan cheese, grated

finely grated rind of ½ lemon

2 tbsp olive oil

salt and pepper

roasted vine tomatoes, to serve

Method

1 Preheat the oven to 220°C/425°F/Gas Mark 7. Cut a deep slit into each chicken breast to make a pocket. Open out the chicken breasts and spread 1 tablespoon of the pesto into each pocket. Fold the chicken flesh back over the pesto and place in an ovenproof dish.

2 Mix the remaining pesto with the breadcrumbs, Parmesan cheese and lemon rind. Spread the breadcrumb mixture over the chicken breasts. Season to taste with salt and pepper, and drizzle with the oil.

3 Bake in the preheated oven for 20 minutes, until the chicken is tender and the juices run clear when a skewer is inserted into the thickest part of the meat.

4 Transfer to warmed serving plates and serve immediately with roasted tomatoes.

MEAT & POULTRY

TURKEY & BARLEY STEW

Serves: 4   **Prep: 10 mins**   **Cook: 33–35 mins**

Ingredients

15 g/½ oz dried ceps

1 onion

450 g/1 lb button mushrooms

4 carrots

2 tbsp olive oil

1 tsp salt

½ tsp pepper

200 g/7 oz barley

600 ml/1 pint vegetable stock, chicken stock or water

1 tbsp fresh thyme leaves

450 g/1 lb turkey breast meat

55 g/2 oz Parmesan cheese, grated

2 tbsp chopped fresh parsley, to garnish

Method

1　Place the ceps in a small bowl and cover with hot water. Dice the onion and slice the mushrooms and carrots. Heat the oil in a large saucepan over a medium–high heat. Add the onion and cook, stirring frequently, for about 4 minutes, until soft. Add the mushrooms and carrots to the pan with the salt and pepper. Cook, stirring occasionally, for a further 4 minutes, until the vegetables are tender. Add the barley and stir to mix well. Add the stock.

2　Remove the ceps from the soaking water, reserving the soaking liquid, and chop. Add to the pan with the soaking liquid and bring to the boil. Meanwhile, finely chop the thyme and add to the pan. Reduce the heat to low and simmer, uncovered, for about 5 minutes.

3　Meanwhile, cut the turkey into 1-cm/½-inch cubes. Add to the stew, stir to mix, then cover and simmer for 15 minutes, until the turkey is cooked through, the barley is tender, and most of the liquid has evaporated. Serve the stew in warmed bowls, garnished with the cheese and parsley.

MEAT & POULTRY

TURKEY CUTLETS WITH PARMA HAM & SAGE

Serves: 2   **Prep: 15 mins**   **Cook: 4–5 mins**

Ingredients

2 skinless, boneless turkey cutlets

2 slices Parma ham, halved

4 fresh sage leaves

2 tbsp plain flour

2 tbsp olive oil

1 tbsp butter

salt and pepper

lemon wedges, to serve

Method

1 Slice the turkey cutlets in half horizontally into two thinner escalopes. Put the escalopes between two sheets of clingfilm and pound lightly with a rolling pin. Season to taste with salt and pepper. Lay half a slice of ham on each escalope, put a sage leaf on top and secure with a cocktail stick.

2 Place the flour in a wide, shallow dish and season to taste with salt and pepper. Dust each side of the escalope with the seasoned flour.

3 Heat the oil in a large frying pan, add the butter and cook until foaming. Add the escalopes and fry over a medium heat for 1½ minutes, sage-side down. Turn the escalopes over and fry for a further 30 seconds, until the turkey is tender and cooked through.

4 Transfer to warmed serving plates, remove the cocktail sticks, and serve immediately with lemon wedges.

CREAMY TURKEY & BROCCOLI GNOCCHI

Serves: 4   **Prep: 15 mins**   **Cook: 8 mins**

Ingredients

1 tbsp sunflower oil

500 g/1 lb 2 oz turkey, cut into strips

2 small leeks, sliced diagonally

500 g/1 lb 2 oz ready-made fresh gnocchi

200 g/7 oz broccoli, cut into bite-sized pieces

85 g/3 oz crème fraîche

1 tbsp wholegrain mustard

3 tbsp orange juice

salt and pepper

3 tbsp toasted pine nuts, to serve

Method

1. Heat the oil in a large frying pan, then add the turkey and leeks, and fry over a high heat for 5–6 minutes.

2. Meanwhile, bring a saucepan of lightly salted water to the boil. Add the gnocchi and broccoli, and cook for 3–4 minutes. Drain the gnocchi and broccoli, and stir into the turkey mixture.

3. Mix together the crème fraîche, mustard and orange juice in a small bowl. Season to taste with salt and pepper, then stir into the turkey mixture.

4. Serve immediately, sprinkled with pine nuts.

HONEYED DUCK

Serves: 4   **Prep: 10-15 minutes   Cook: 6-8 minutes**

Ingredients

4 skinless duck breasts

1 tbsp olive oil

bunch of spring onions, trimmed and sliced

1 small head Chinese leaves, finely shredded

salt and pepper

Marinade

2 tbsp clear honey

4 tbsp soy sauce

Method

1 Slice the duck into thin strips and place in a shallow dish. Combine the marinade ingredients and pour over the duck.

2 Heat a wok over a medium-high heat, then add the oil. Add the duck strips (reserving the marinade) and cook for 2 minutes until browned.

3 Add the spring onions, Chinese leaves and the reserved marinade. Cook for 3-4 minutes, until the duck is cooked but still a little pink in the centre.

4 Season to taste with salt and pepper and serve immediately.

MOROCCAN MEATBALLS WITH MINT YOGURT

Serves: 4   **Prep: 20–25 mins**   **Cook: 15 mins**

Ingredients

olive oil spray
½ small onion
1 garlic clove
450 g/1 lb fresh lamb mince
1½ tsp ground cumin
1 tsp salt
½ tsp pepper
¼ tsp ground cinnamon
1 egg
10 g/¼ oz fresh breadcrumbs
4 pitta breads, to serve

Mint yogurt

10 g/¼ oz fresh mint leaves
280 g/10 oz natural yogurt
juice of ½ lemon
½ tsp salt
⅛ tsp cayenne pepper

Salad

1 cucumber
140 g/5 oz cherry tomatoes
juice of 1 lemon
2 tbsp chopped fresh flat-leaf parsley
½ tsp salt

Method

1 Preheat the oven to 190°C/375°F/Gas Mark 5 and spray a large baking sheet with oil. Finely chop the onion and garlic. Put the lamb, onion, garlic, cumin, salt, pepper, cinnamon, egg and breadcrumbs into a large bowl, mix well to combine and form into 2.5-cm/1-inch balls. Place the meatballs on the prepared baking sheet and spray with oil. Bake in the preheated oven for about 15 minutes, until cooked through.

2 Meanwhile, wrap the pitta breads in foil and put them in the oven. To make the mint yogurt, finely chop the mint and put in a small bowl with the remaining ingredients. Stir to combine. To make the salad, dice the cucumber and halve the tomatoes. Put them into a medium-sized bowl and mix to combine. Add the lemon juice, parsley and salt, and stir to combine.

3 Remove the meatballs and bread from the oven. Cut the pitta breads in half. Stuff a few meatballs into each half and spoon in some of the mint yogurt. Serve two halves per person with the salad on the side.

QUICK SPAGHETTI BOLOGNESE

Serves: 4   **Prep: 15 mins**   **Cook: 30 mins**

Ingredients

2 tbsp olive oil

1 large onion, chopped

500 g/1 lb 2 oz lean beef mince

1 green pepper, deseeded and chopped

1 garlic clove, crushed

150 ml/5 fl oz red wine or beef stock

400 g/14 oz canned chopped plum tomatoes

2 tbsp tomato purée

1 tbsp dried oregano

200 g/7 oz dried spaghetti

salt and pepper

freshly grated Parmesan cheese, to serve

Method

1 Heat the oil in a large saucepan over a high heat. Add the onion and mince, and fry, stirring, until lightly browned with no remaining traces of pink. Stir in the green pepper and garlic.

2 Add the wine, tomatoes, tomato purée and oregano. Bring to the boil and boil rapidly for 2 minutes. Reduce the heat, cover and simmer for 20 minutes, stirring occasionally.

3 Meanwhile, bring a large saucepan of lightly salted water to the boil, add the spaghetti, bring back to the boil and cook for about 8–10 minutes, until tender but still firm to the bite. Drain the spaghetti in a colander and return to the pan.

4 Season the sauce to taste with salt and pepper, then stir into the spaghetti. Serve immediately, with Parmesan cheese.

MEAT & POULTRY

SPEEDY BEEF STEW

Serves: 4 **Prep: 15 mins** **Cook: 30 mins**

Ingredients

900 g/2 lb beef, finely sliced

3 tbsp plain flour

2 tbsp olive oil

1 large onion

2 garlic cloves

225 ml/8 fl oz red wine

450 g/1 lb button mushrooms

450 g/1 lb new potatoes

4 carrots

2 celery sticks

1 tbsp fresh thyme leaves

700 ml/1¼ pints beef stock

3 tbsp tomato purée

2 tbsp chopped fresh parsley

salt and pepper

crusty bread, to serve

Method

1 Season the beef with ½ teaspoon of salt and ½ teaspoon of pepper. Toss in the flour. Heat the oil in a large, heavy-based saucepan over a medium–high heat. Add the meat and cook, stirring frequently, for about 4 minutes, until brown all over. Meanwhile, dice the onion and finely chop the garlic. Add to the pan and cook for 2–3 minutes, until the onion begins to soften. Add the wine and bring to the boil, scraping up any sediment from the base of the pan.

2 Meanwhile, quarter the mushrooms and dice the potatoes, carrots and celery. Finely chop the thyme. Add the vegetables to the pan with 1 teaspoon of salt, ½ teaspoon of pepper, the stock, tomato purée and thyme. Bring to the boil, then reduce the heat to low, cover, and simmer for about 15 minutes, until the vegetables are tender.

3 Remove the lid of the pan and continue to simmer for a further 5 minutes until the sauce is slightly thickened. Stir the parsley into the pan and serve the stew hot, with crusty bread for mopping up the sauce.

MEAT & POULTRY

CLASSIC BURGERS

Serves: 4 **Prep: 15 mins** **Cook: 10–12 mins**

Ingredients

750 g/1 lb 10 oz fresh
beef mince

1 beef stock cube

1 tbsp minced dried onion

2 tbsp water

2 large tomatoes, skinned,
deseeded and chopped

1 tbsp chopped fresh basil

55 g/2 oz Cheddar cheese,
grated

sprigs of fresh basil,
to garnish

To serve

4 burger buns, halved

mustard

tomato ketchup

Method

1 Preheat the grill to medium–high. Place the beef in a large mixing bowl. Crumble the stock cube over the mixture and add the dried onion, water, tomatoes and the chopped basil, and mix well.

2 Divide the meat into four portions, shape each into a ball, then flatten slightly to make a burger of your preferred thickness.

3 Cook the burgers under the preheated grill for 5–6 minutes. Turn the burgers, sprinkle cheese over the top and cook for a further 5–6 minutes, until cooked through.

4 Place the burgers on the bottom halves of the buns and top with the lids. Garnish with sprigs of basil and serve immediately with mustard and tomato ketchup.

MEAT & POULTRY

HOT SESAME BEEF

Serves: 4 **Prep: 15 mins** **Cook: 13-15 mins**

Ingredients

200 g/7 oz basmati rice
500 g/1 lb 2 oz fillet steak
1½ tbsp sesame seeds
2 garlic cloves
125 ml/4 fl oz beef stock
2 tbsp soy sauce
2 tbsp grated fresh ginger
1 tsp cornflour
½ tsp chilli flakes
3 tbsp sesame oil
1 large head of broccoli
1 yellow pepper, deseeded and thinly sliced
1 fresh red chilli, finely sliced
1 tbsp chilli oil, or to taste
salt and pepper
1 tbsp chopped fresh coriander, to garnish

Method

1 Cook the rice in a saucepan of lightly salted water for 10–12 minutes, until tender. Drain.

2 Meanwhile, cut the beef into thin strips and mix with 1 tablespoon of the sesame seeds in a bowl.

3 Finely chop the garlic and place in a separate bowl with the stock, soy sauce, ginger, cornflour and chilli flakes.

4 Preheat a wok or large frying pan over a high heat. Add 1 tablespoon of the sesame oil and heat until very hot. Add the beef and stir-fry until starting to brown. Remove and set aside, then wipe the wok clean with kitchen paper.

5 Heat the remaining sesame oil in the wok. Cut the broccoli into florets and add to the wok with the yellow pepper, red chilli and chilli oil, and stir-fry for 2–3 minutes. Stir in the stock mixture, cover and simmer for 2 minutes.

6 Return the beef to the wok and simmer until the juices thicken, stirring occasionally. Cook for a further 1–2 minutes. Sprinkle with the remaining sesame seeds and season to taste with salt and pepper.

7 Transfer the rice to warmed serving bowls and top with the beef and vegetables. Garnish with chopped coriander and serve immediately.

MEAT & POULTRY

STEAK WITH CHIMICHURRI

Serves: 4

Prep: 15–20 mins

Cook: 15 mins,
plus resting

Ingredients

675–900 g/1 lb 8 oz–2 lb
sirloin steak

4 fresh corn cobs

1 shallot

3 garlic cloves

4 tbsp sherry vinegar or red
wine vinegar

60 g/2¼ oz fresh
flat-leaf parsley

1 tbsp fresh oregano leaves

½ tsp crushed red
pepper flakes

125 ml/4 fl oz olive oil

juice of 1 lemon

salt and pepper

Method

1 Preheat the grill to medium–high. Generously season the steak with salt and pepper. Remove the corn husks and silks, then wrap individually in foil.

2 To make the sauce, finely chop the shallot and garlic and place in a small bowl with the vinegar and 1 teaspoon of salt. Finely chop the parsley and oregano, and add them to the vinegar mixture along with the red pepper flakes. Whisk in the oil until well combined. Stir in the lemon juice. Put the corn and the steak on the grill rack. Cook the steak, turning once, for about 4 minutes per side for medium-rare, until nicely seared on the outside. Turn the corn occasionally, cooking it for 15 minutes in total. Once cooked, remove from the grill and cut each cob in half.

3 Transfer the meat to a chopping board and leave to rest for 4 minutes. Slice it against the grain into 5-mm/¼-inch thick slices. Serve the meat drizzled with the sauce, and the corn on the side.

ORANGE & LEMON CRISPY LAMB CUTLETS

Serves: 2   **Prep: 10 mins**   **Cook: 10–12 mins**

Ingredients

1 garlic clove, crushed

1 tbsp olive oil

2 tbsp finely grated orange rind

2 tbsp finely grated lemon rind

6 lamb cutlets

salt and pepper

orange wedges, to garnish

Method

1 Place the garlic, oil and citrus rinds in a bowl. Season to taste with salt and pepper, and mix together. Brush over the lamb cutlets.

2 Preheat a ridged grill pan over a high heat. Add the cutlets to the hot pan and cook for 4–5 minutes on each side.

3 Transfer to warmed serving plates. Garnish with orange wedges and serve immediately.

LAMB & FETA BURGERS

Makes: 4-6

Prep: 15 mins,
plus chilling

Cook: 12 mins

Ingredients

450 g/1 lb fresh lamb mince

225 g/8 oz feta cheese, crumbled

2 garlic cloves, crushed

6 spring onions, finely chopped

85 g/3 oz ready-to-eat prunes, chopped

25 g/1 oz pine nuts, toasted

55 g/2 oz fresh wholemeal breadcrumbs

1 tbsp chopped fresh rosemary

1 tbsp sunflower oil

salt and pepper

4-6 burger buns, split

Method

1 Place the lamb mince in a large bowl with the feta, garlic, spring onions, prunes, pine nuts and breadcrumbs. Mix well, breaking up any lumps.

2 Add the rosemary to the lamb mixture with salt and pepper to taste. Mix together, then shape into four to six equal-sized patties. Cover and leave to chill in the refrigerator for 30 minutes.

3 Heat a ridged grill pan over a medium–high heat. Brush the burgers lightly with half the oil and cook in the pan for 4 minutes, then brush with the remaining oil and turn over. Cook for a further 4 minutes, or until cooked through. Place the burgers in the buns and serve immediately.

LAMB KOFTAS WITH YOGURT, THYME & LEMON DIP

Serves: 4   **Prep: 20 mins**   **Cook: 12–14 mins**

Ingredients

500 g/1 lb 2 oz lean lamb mince

25 g/1 oz fresh white breadcrumbs

1 onion, grated

1 garlic clove, crushed

1 tsp ground coriander

1 tsp ground cumin

2 tbsp chopped fresh mint

olive oil, for brushing

salt and pepper

lemon wedges, to serve

Yogurt, thyme & lemon dip

150 ml/5 fl oz natural yogurt

finely grated rind and juice of ½ lemon

1 tbsp chopped fresh thyme

salt and pepper

Method

1 Put the mince, breadcrumbs, onion, garlic, coriander, cumin and mint into a bowl and mix together. Season well with salt and pepper.

2 Divide the mixture into eight equal portions and press evenly onto eight pre-soaked wooden skewers or metal skewers.

3 To make the yogurt, thyme and lemon dip, put the yogurt and lemon rind and juice into a bowl and mix together. Stir in the thyme and season to taste with salt and pepper.

4 Heat a ridged grill pan over a medium–high heat. Brush the koftas with oil, place in the pan and cook, turning occasionally, for 10–12 minutes, until golden brown and cooked through. Serve with the thyme and lemon dip, and lemon wedges.

HAM & LEEK RISOTTO

Serves: 4   **Prep: 10 mins**   **Cook: 33–35 mins**

Ingredients

380 g/13¼ oz arborio rice

1 litre/1¾ pints water

1 shallot

2 leeks, white and light green parts only

350 g/12 oz cooked ham

30 g/1 oz fresh parsley, plus extra to garnish

2 tbsp olive oil

4 tbsp dry white wine

1 litre/1¾ pints chicken stock, plus extra if needed

145 g/5¼ oz fresh or frozen peas

30 g/1 oz butter

60 g/2¼ oz grated Parmesan cheese, plus extra to garnish

salt

Method

1 Rinse the rice under cold running water. Place in a large saucepan with the water and a generous pinch of salt. Bring to the boil over a high heat, then reduce the heat to low and simmer, uncovered, for 7 minutes. Meanwhile, dice the shallot and trim and dice the leeks. Dice the ham. Finely chop the parsley. Drain the rice in a colander and set aside.

2 Heat the oil in the pan used to cook the rice. Add the ham, shallot and leeks, and cook, stirring, for about 3 minutes, until the vegetables begin to soften and the ham begins to brown. Add the wine and cook for a further 1–2 minutes. Add the rice, stock and ¼–½ teaspoon of salt, and bring to the boil. Reduce the heat to medium and simmer, stirring occasionally, for 12 minutes, or until most of the stock has evaporated.

3 Taste the risotto. If it is not yet cooked through, add a little more stock and cook for a few more minutes. Stir in the peas in the last couple of minutes of cooking. Stir the butter and cheese into the risotto. Garnish with cheese and parsley, and serve immediately.

SPAGHETTI WITH BACON & CRISPY BREADCRUMBS

Serves: 2   **Prep: 15 mins**   **Cook: 13–15 mins**

Ingredients

55 g/2 oz day-old ciabatta bread (approximately one roll)

175 g/6 oz dried spaghetti

2 tsp olive oil

140 g/5 oz smoked streaky bacon, chopped

sprig of fresh rosemary, crushed

15 g/½ oz butter

40 g/1½ oz pine nuts

2 garlic cloves, crushed

2–3 tbsp chopped fresh flat-leaf parsley

salt and pepper

Method

1 Put the bread, including any crusts, in a food processor or blender and process until the mixture resembles coarse breadcrumbs.

2 Bring a large saucepan of lightly salted water to the boil. Add the pasta, bring back to the boil and cook for 8–10 minutes, until tender but still firm to the bite. Drain.

3 Meanwhile, heat the oil in a large frying pan, add the bacon and rosemary and fry for 2–3 minutes, until the bacon is golden brown. Remove from the pan with a slotted spoon and set aside.

4 Add the butter to the remaining bacon fat in the pan. When melted, add the breadcrumbs, pine nuts and garlic. Fry for 2–3 minutes, stirring until golden brown. Combine the breadcrumb mixture with the pasta, bacon and rosemary. Add the parsley and season to taste with pepper.

5 Transfer to warmed serving bowls and serve immediately.

PARMA HAM & RED PEPPER PIZZA

Makes: 1 Pizza   **Prep: 15 mins**   **Cook: 10 mins**

Ingredients

2 tbsp olive oil

30-cm/12-inch ready-made pizza base

4 tbsp ready-made red pesto sauce

1 small red pepper, deseeded and thinly sliced

4 thin slices Parma ham

100 g/3½ oz cherry plum tomatoes, halved

100 g/3½ oz mozzarella cheese, torn into pieces

1 tsp dried oregano

salt and pepper

Method

1. Preheat the oven to 220°C/425°F/Gas Mark 7. Brush a large baking sheet with a little oil and place the pizza base on the sheet.

2. Spread the pesto sauce over the pizza base to within 1-cm/½-inch of the edge. Arrange the red pepper slices, ham and tomatoes over the pizza.

3. Scatter with the mozzarella, oregano, and salt and pepper to taste, then drizzle over the remaining olive oil.

4. Bake the pizza in the preheated oven for about 10 minutes, until bubbling and golden. Serve immediately.

ITALIAN SAUSAGE SUBS

Makes: 4　　　**Prep: 10–15 mins**　　　**Cook: 30 mins**

Ingredients

2 tbsp olive oil

8 Italian sausages

1 green pepper

1 red pepper

1 orange pepper

1 onion

2 garlic cloves

½ tsp salt

½ tsp pepper

125 ml/4 fl oz red wine

400 g/14 oz canned chopped tomatoes

2 tsp dried oregano

4 submarine rolls

280 g/10 oz rocket, to serve

salad dressing, to serve

mayonnaise, to serve

Method

1　Heat the oil in a large frying pan over a medium–high heat. Add the sausages and cook, turning occasionally, for 6–8 minutes, until brown all over. Remove from the pan and set aside. Meanwhile, deseed the green, red and orange peppers and slice them into 2.5-cm/1-inch wide strips. Halve the onion and thinly slice into half circles. Finely chop the garlic.

2　Add the vegetables to the pan and cook, stirring frequently, for about 4 minutes, until they begin to soften, then add the garlic, salt and pepper. Cook, stirring, for a further 1–2 minutes. Add the wine, tomatoes and oregano, and bring to the boil. Return the sausages to the pan, cover and cook for about 15 minutes, until the sausages are cooked through.

3　Split the rolls and spoon some vegetables into each. Place two sausages on top and serve hot with rocket, salad dressing and mayonnaise on the side.

CHORIZO, CHILLI & CHICKPEA CASSEROLE

Serves: 20–25   **Prep: 15 mins**   **Cook: 20 mins**

Ingredients

2 tbsp olive oil

1 onion, sliced

1 large yellow pepper, deseeded and sliced

1 garlic clove, crushed

1 tsp chilli flakes

225 g/8 oz chorizo sausage

400 g/14 oz canned chopped tomatoes

400 g/14 oz canned chickpeas, drained

200 g/7 oz basmati rice

handful of rocket leaves

salt and pepper

4 tbsp roughly chopped fresh basil, to garnish

Method

1 Heat the oil in a large, ovenproof casserole over a medium heat. Add the onion and cook for 5 minutes, stirring occasionally.

2 Add the yellow pepper, garlic and chilli flakes, and cook for 2 minutes, stirring. Chop the chorizo into bite-sized chunks and stir into the casserole.

3 Add the tomatoes and chickpeas with salt and pepper to taste. Bring to the boil, cover and simmer for 10 minutes.

4 Meanwhile, cook the rice in a saucepan of lightly salted boiling water for 10–12 minutes, until tender. Drain.

5 Stir the rocket into the casserole. Transfer to warmed serving bowls. Garnish with fresh basil and serve immediately with the rice.

MEAT & POULTRY

PORK & APPLE ONE POT

Serves: 4 **Prep: 15 mins** **Cook: 30 mins**

Ingredients

1 onion

4 smoked bacon rashers

675 g/1 lb 8 oz boneless pork shoulder

30 g/1 oz plain flour

2 tbsp vegetable oil

2 large green apples, such as Granny Smith

350 g/12 oz baby new potatoes

225 g/8 oz shredded green cabbage

1 tbsp fresh thyme leaves

1 tbsp white wine vinegar

450 ml/16 fl oz chicken stock

225 ml/8 fl oz apple juice

2 tbsp Dijon mustard

salt and pepper

Method

1 Dice the onion and bacon. Cut the pork into small cubes. Place the flour in a large polythene bag and season the pork with 1 teaspoon of salt and ½ teaspoon of pepper. Put the meat in the bag with the flour, close the top and shake to coat well.

2 Heat the oil in a large, heavy-based saucepan over a medium–high heat. Add the onion and bacon and cook, stirring, for about 3 minutes, until the onion begins to soften and the bacon begins to brown. Add the pork and cook, stirring occasionally, until the meat is brown all over. Transfer the mixture to a bowl. Meanwhile, core and dice the apples and dice the potatoes.

3 Add the apple, potatoes, cabbage and thyme to the pan along with the vinegar, stock and apple juice. Add the mustard, ½ teaspoon of salt and ¼ teaspoon of pepper, bring to the boil, then reduce the heat to a simmer. Return the pork, onion and bacon to the pot and cook, uncovered, for about 15 minutes, until the meat is cooked through. Serve immediately.

GINGER PORK WITH SHIITAKE MUSHROOMS

Serves: 4   **Prep: 15 mins**   **Cook: 9–12 mins**

Ingredients

2 tbsp vegetable oil

3 shallots, finely chopped

2 garlic cloves, crushed

5-cm/2-inch piece fresh ginger, thinly sliced

500 g/1 lb 2 oz pork, cut into strips

250 g/9 oz shiitake mushrooms, sliced

4 tbsp soy sauce

4 tbsp rice wine

1 tsp light muscovado sugar

1 tsp cornflour

2 tbsp cold water

3 tbsp chopped fresh coriander, to garnish

Method

1 Heat a wok over a high heat, then add the oil. Add the shallots and stir-fry for 2–3 minutes, then add the garlic and ginger, and stir-fry for 1 minute.

2 Add the pork strips and stir-fry for a further minute, then add the mushrooms and stir-fry for 2–3 minutes, until the pork is cooked through.

3 Stir in the soy sauce, rice wine and sugar. Blend the cornflour and water until smooth, add to the pan, stirring, and cook until the juices are thick and clear. Transfer to warmed serving dishes and serve garnished with coriander.

SPICY PORK MEATBALLS

Serves: 4   **Prep: 15–20 mins**   **Cook: 13–15 mins**

Ingredients

675 g/1 lb 8 oz lean pork mince

1 garlic clove, finely chopped

1 tsp ground ginger

pinch of ground cloves

½ tsp freshly grated nutmeg

½ tsp ground allspice

2 egg yolks

40 g/1½ oz ground almonds

oil, for shallow-frying

salt and pepper

mixed salad leaves and crusty bread, to serve

Method

1 Place the pork in a large mixing bowl. Add the garlic, spices, egg yolks and ground almonds. Season to taste with salt and pepper, and mix together. Use a small ice-cream scoop to shape the mixture into small balls.

2 Heat a shallow depth of oil in a deep frying pan until very hot. Add the meatballs in batches and fry, for 8–10 minutes, until cooked through.

3 Lift out the meatballs with a slotted spoon and drain on absorbent kitchen paper.

4 Transfer to warmed serving plates and serve immediately with salad leaves and crusty bread.

PORK PAD THAI

Serves: 4   **Prep: 25 mins**   **Cook: 7–10 mins**

Ingredients

225 g/8 oz thick dried rice noodles

2 tbsp groundnut or vegetable oil

4 spring onions, roughly chopped

2 garlic cloves, crushed

2 red chillies, deseeded and sliced

225 g/8 oz pork fillet, trimmed and thinly sliced

115 g/4 oz large prawns, cooked and peeled

juice of 1 lime

2 tbsp Thai fish sauce

2 eggs, beaten

55 g/2 oz fresh beansprouts

handful of chopped fresh coriander

55 g/2 oz unsalted peanuts, chopped

lime wedges, to serve

Method

1 Soak the noodles in a large saucepan of boiling water, covered, for 10 minutes until just tender, or according to the packet instructions. Drain, rinse under cold running water and set aside.

2 Preheat a wok or large frying pan over a high heat. Add the oil and heat until very hot. Add the spring onions, garlic and chillies, and stir-fry over a medium–high heat for 1–2 minutes. Add the pork and stir-fry over a high heat for 1–2 minutes until browned all over.

3 Add the prawns, lime juice, fish sauce and eggs, and stir-fry over a medium heat for 2–3 minutes, until the eggs have set and the prawns are heated through.

4 Add the beansprouts, most of the coriander, the peanuts and the noodles, and stir-fry for 30 seconds to heat through.

5 Transfer to warmed serving bowls. Garnish with the remaining coriander and serve immediately with lime wedges.

★ Variation

These fiery flavours are staples in Thai cooking. Try replacing the pork with chicken for another classic combination.

MEAT & POULTRY

FISH & SEAFOOD

RUSTIC FISH CASSEROLE

Serves: 4 **Prep: 15 mins** **Cook: 11–13 mins**

Ingredients

300 g/10½ oz live clams, scrubbed

2 tbsp olive oil

1 large onion, chopped

2 garlic cloves, crushed

2 celery sticks, sliced

350 g/12 oz firm white fish fillet

250 g/9 oz prepared squid rings

400 ml/14 fl oz fish stock

6 plum tomatoes, chopped

small bunch of fresh thyme

salt and pepper

crusty bread, to serve

Method

1 Discard any clams with broken shells and any that refuse to close when tapped.

2 Heat the oil in a large frying pan over a medium heat. Add the onion, garlic and celery, and cook for 3–4 minutes, stirring occasionally, until softened but not browned. Meanwhile, cut the fish into chunks.

3 Stir the fish and squid into the pan, then fry gently for 2 minutes. Stir in the stock, tomatoes and thyme with salt and pepper to taste. Cover and simmer gently for 3–4 minutes. Add the clams, cover and cook over a high heat for a further 2 minutes, or until the shells open. Discard any that remain closed.

4 Transfer to warmed serving bowls and serve immediately with crusty bread.

★ Variation

If you can't get hold of clams, mussels are a great substitution. Their rich, buttery flavour will work well with the freshness of the tomatoes.

QUICK & CREAMY FISH GRATIN

Serves: 4   **Prep: 15 mins**   **Cook: 20–23 mins**

Ingredients

1 tbsp olive oil

2 shallots, finely chopped

150 ml/5 fl oz dry white wine or fish stock

1 bay leaf

200 g/7 oz closed cup mushrooms, thickly sliced

100 g/3½ oz crème fraîche

500 g/1 lb 2 oz white fish fillets, cut into chunks

175 g/6 oz prawns, cooked and peeled

175 g/6 oz frozen peas

40 g/1½ oz butter

150 g/5½ oz fresh white breadcrumbs

salt and pepper

chopped fresh parsley, to garnish

Method

1 Heat the oil in an ovenproof saucepan or a shallow, flameproof casserole and fry the shallots. Cook for 2–3 minutes, stirring occasionally, until softened. Add the wine, bay leaf and mushrooms, and simmer for 2 minutes, stirring occasionally.

2 Stir in the crème fraîche and add the fish. Season to taste with salt and pepper. Bring to the boil, cover and simmer for 5–6 minutes, until the fish is almost cooked. Preheat the grill to medium.

3 Remove and discard the bay leaf, then add the prawns and peas, and bring back to the boil.

4 Meanwhile, melt the butter in a separate saucepan and stir in the breadcrumbs. Spread the breadcrumb mixture evenly over the top of the fish mixture.

5 Place the saucepan under the preheated grill for 3–4 minutes, until the topping is golden brown and bubbling.

6 Transfer to warmed serving plates. Garnish with parsley and serve immediately.

PEPPERED TUNA STEAKS

Serves: 4   **Prep: 10–15 mins**   **Cook: 6–8 mins**

Ingredients

4 tuna steaks, about 175 g/6 oz each

4 tsp sunflower or olive oil

1 tsp salt

2 tbsp pink, green and black peppercorns, roughly crushed

handful of fresh rocket leaves, to garnish

lemon wedges, to serve

Method

1 Brush the tuna steaks with the oil and sprinkle with the salt. Coat the fish in the crushed peppercorns, lightly pressing them into the surface of the fish.

2 Heat a ridged griddle pan over a medium heat. Add the tuna and cook for 2–3 minutes on each side.

3 Garnish with rocket and serve with lemon wedges for squeezing over.

TUNA NOODLE CASSEROLE

Serves: 4   **Prep: 15 mins**   **Cook: 26–28 mins**

Ingredients

1 onion
1 carrot
1 tbsp olive oil
140 g/5 oz button mushrooms
450 ml/16 fl oz chicken or vegetable stock
300 ml/10 fl oz canned condensed cream of mushroom soup
475 g/1 lb 1 oz canned tuna in brine
350 g/12 oz dried egg noodles
125 g/4½ oz panko breadcrumbs
55 g/2 oz freshly grated Parmesan cheese
salt and pepper

Method

1 Preheat the oven to 200°C/400°F/Gas Mark 6. Dice the onion and carrot. Heat the oil in a large, ovenproof frying pan or wide saucepan. Add the onion and carrot and cook, stirring occasionally. Meanwhile, slice the mushrooms and add them to the pan. Add salt and pepper to taste and cook, stirring occasionally, for 2–3 minutes, until the vegetables begin to soften.

2 Stir in the stock and soup, and bring to the boil. Drain the tuna and add it to the pan, breaking up any big chunks. Add the noodles and stir to coat with the sauce. Cover the pan and transfer to the preheated oven for about 15 minutes, until the noodles are tender. Preheat the grill to medium.

3 Remove the pan from the oven and stir the casserole well. Sprinkle the breadcrumbs and cheese evenly over the top, then place under the grill for 2–3 minutes, until the topping is golden brown. Serve immediately.

GRIDDLED TUNA WITH LEMON, CAPERS & THYME

Serves: 4   **Prep: 10-15 mins**   **Cook: 11-17 mins**

Ingredients

4 tuna steaks, about 175 g/6 oz each

4 tbsp olive oil

finely grated rind and juice of 1 lemon

3 tbsp salted capers, rinsed

2 tbsp chopped fresh thyme

salt and pepper

lemon wedges, to serve

Method

1 Brush the tuna steaks with 1 tablespoon of the oil and season to taste with salt and pepper.

2 Place the remaining oil, the lemon rind and juice, capers and thyme in a small pan over a low heat.

3 Heat a ridged griddle pan until hot, then cook the tuna, in batches if necessary, for 2–3 minutes on each side.

4 Bring the lemon and caper mixture to the boil and spoon over the tuna.

5 Transfer to warmed serving plates and serve immediately with lemon wedges.

SPICY TUNA FISHCAKES

Serves: 4

Prep: 15 mins

Cook: 7-10 mins

Ingredients

200 g/7 oz canned tuna in oil, drained

200 g/7 oz mashed potato

2-3 tbsp curry paste

1 spring onion, trimmed and finely chopped

1 egg, beaten

4 tbsp plain flour, plus extra for shaping

sunflower or groundnut oil, for frying

salt and pepper

rocket leaves and lemon wedges, to serve

Method

1 Place the tuna in a large mixing bowl. Add the mashed potato, curry paste, spring onion and egg. Season to taste with salt and pepper, and mix together.

2 Divide the mixture into four portions and shape each into a ball. Then, on a floured surface, flatten slightly to make a patty shape of your preferred thickness. Season the flour to taste with salt and pepper. Dust each patty in the seasoned flour.

3 Heat the oil in a large frying pan, add the patties and fry, for 3-4 minutes on each side, until crisp and golden.

4 Transfer to warmed serving plates and serve immediately with rocket leaves and lemon wedges.

FISH & SEAFOOD

BAKED LEMON COD WITH HERB SAUCE

Serves: 4   **Prep: 15–20 mins**   **Cook: 20 mins**

Ingredients

4 thick cod fillets

olive oil, for brushing

8 thin lemon slices

salt and pepper

cooked French beans, to serve

Herb sauce

4 tbsp olive oil

1 garlic clove, crushed

4 tbsp chopped fresh parsley

2 tbsp chopped fresh mint

juice of ½ lemon

salt and pepper

Method

1 Preheat the oven to 200°C/400°F/Gas Mark 6. Rinse each cod fillet and pat dry with kitchen paper, then brush with oil. Place each fillet on a piece of baking paper large enough to encase the fish in a parcel. Top each fillet with two lemon slices and season to taste with salt and pepper. Fold over the baking paper to encase the fish and bake in the preheated oven for 20 minutes, or until just cooked and opaque.

2 Meanwhile, to make the herb sauce, put all the ingredients, including salt and pepper to taste, into a food processor or blender and process until finely chopped.

3 Carefully unfold each parcel and place on a serving plate. Pour a spoonful of herb sauce over each piece of fish before serving, accompanied by French beans.

FISH & SEAFOOD

BAKED 'FISH & CHIPS'

Serves: 4   **Prep: 15 mins**   **Cook: 30 mins**

Ingredients

675 g/1 lb 8 oz potatoes

2 tbsp vegetable oil

675 g/1 lb 8 oz cod fillet

30 g/1 oz plain flour

2 large egg whites

200 g/7 oz panko breadcrumbs

vegetable oil cooking spray

salt and pepper

tartare sauce, to serve

Salad

1 small cucumber

4–6 radishes

280 g/10 oz washed mixed baby salad leaves

1 lemon

1 tsp white wine vinegar

½ teaspoon salt

¼ teaspoon pepper

pinch of sugar

4 tbsp olive oil

Method

1 Preheat the oven to 230°/450°F/Gas Mark 8. Scrub the potatoes and cut them into 5-cm/2–inch chips. Rinse the potatoes with cold water and then pat very dry with kitchen paper. Spread the potatoes on a baking sheet in a single layer and toss with the vegetable oil. Season with ½ teaspoon of salt and bake in the preheated oven for about 25 minutes.

2 Meanwhile, cut the fish into strips and season it on both sides with ½ teaspoon of salt and ¼ teaspoon of pepper. Place the flour, egg whites and breadcrumbs in three separate shallow bowls. Beat the egg whites until they are frothy. Dip the fish in the flour, then in the egg whites, and roll in the breadcrumbs until completely coated. Remove the chips from the oven and push them to one side of the baking sheet. Arrange the fish on the other side in a single layer and spritz with the oil spray. Return the baking sheet to the oven and bake for 15 minutes, turning the fish once, until the fish is crisp and cooked through, and the potatoes are brown.

3 Meanwhile, make the salad. Slice the cucumber and radishes, place in a large salad bowl with the salad leaves and toss together. Zest and juice the lemon and combine with the vinegar, salt, pepper and sugar in another small bowl. Whisk in the oil until well combined, then dress the salad. Serve the fish and chips with a dollop of tartare sauce for dipping and the salad on the side.

MEDITERRANEAN SOLE WITH OLIVES & TOMATOES

Serves: 4   **Prep: 15–20 mins**   **Cook: 20 mins**

Ingredients

1 shallot

1 garlic clove

1 fennel bulb, plus fennel fronds to garnish

35 g/1¼ oz stoned Kalamata olives

2 tbsp olive oil

125 g/4½ oz uncooked couscous

240 g/8¾ oz drained canned, chopped tomatoes

350 ml/12 fl oz vegetable stock or water

4 x 175-g/6-oz sole fillets

¼–½ tsp crushed chilli flakes

1 tbsp fresh oregano leaves or 1 tsp dried oregano

60 g/2¼ oz butter

50 ml/2 fl oz white wine

salt and pepper

Method

1 Chop the shallot and finely chop the garlic. Trim, core and thinly slice the fennel. Chop the olives. Heat the oil in a large frying pan over a medium–high heat. Add the shallot, garlic and fennel, and cook, stirring occasionally, for about 3 minutes, until the vegetables are soft. Add the couscous, tomatoes, stock, olives and 1 teaspoon of salt. Stir to combine.

2 Lay the fish fillets on top of the couscous mixture, in a single layer if possible. Season with salt and pepper. Sprinkle the chilli flakes and oregano over the fish. Cut the butter into small pieces and scatter it over the fish. Drizzle the wine over and around the fish.

3 Cover, reduce the heat to low, and cook for about 15 minutes, until the fish is cooked through and the couscous is tender. Serve immediately on warmed plates garnished with fennel fronds.

SALMON FILLETS WITH PESTO

Serves: 4   **Prep: 10 mins**   **Cook: 10-15 mins**

Ingredients

4 salmon steaks,
about 175 g/6 oz each

mixed salad and griddled
ciabatta, to serve

Parsley pesto

2 garlic cloves,
coarsely chopped

25 g/1 oz pine nuts

40 g/1½ oz fresh parsley,
coarse stems removed

1 tsp salt

25 g/1 oz freshly grated
Parmesan cheese

125–150 ml/4–5 fl oz
extra virgin olive oil

Method

1 To make the parsley pesto, put the garlic, pine nuts, parsley and salt into a food processor or blender, and process to a purée. Add the Parmesan and blend briefly again. Then add 125 ml/4 fl oz oil and blend again. If the consistency is too thick, add the remaining oil and blend again until smooth. Scrape into a bowl and set aside. Preheat the grill to medium.

2 Cook the salmon under the preheated grill for 10–15 minutes, depending on the thickness of the fillets, until the flesh turns pink and flakes easily.

3 Transfer to serving plates, top with the parsley pesto and serve immediately with salad and ciabatta.

SALMON & POTATO TRAYBAKE

Serves: 4   **Prep: 20 mins**   **Cook: 20–22 mins**

Ingredients

450 g/1 lb new potatoes

2 tbsp olive oil, plus extra for oiling

1 tsp salt

350 g/12 oz Brussels sprouts

½ tsp pepper

675 g/1 lb 8 oz salmon fillet

2 tbsp unsalted butter

1 tbsp fresh dill, plus extra sprigs to garnish

juice of 1 lemon, plus lemon halves to serve

3 spring onions

Method

1 Preheat the oven to 230°C/450°F/Gas Mark 8 and oil a large baking dish. Slice the potatoes into thin rounds and place them in the base of the dish in an even layer. Drizzle half the oil evenly over the potatoes, then sprinkle with half the salt. Place in the preheated oven.

2 Trim and thinly slice the sprouts. Put them into a medium-sized bowl and toss with the remaining oil, half the remaining salt and the pepper. Remove the dish from the oven and spread the sliced sprouts over the top of the potatoes in an even layer. Return to the oven. Cut the salmon into 5-cm/2-inch chunks and season with the remaining salt. Put the butter into a small bowl and melt in the microwave. Finely chop the dill and add it to the butter with the lemon juice. Trim and slice the spring onions.

3 Remove the dish from the oven and place the salmon pieces on top of the vegetables. Spoon the butter mixture over the salmon pieces and drizzle any remaining mixture over the vegetables. Scatter the spring onions over the top. Return to the oven and bake for 10–12 minutes, until the salmon flakes easily with a fork and is cooked through. Serve immediately with lemon halves for squeezing over and garnished with dill sprigs.

SMOKED SALMON TAGLIATELLE

Serves: 4   **Prep: 10-15 mins**   **Cook: 13-15 mins**

Ingredients

350 g/12 oz dried tagliatelle

2 tbsp olive oil

1 garlic clove,
finely chopped

115 g/4 oz smoked salmon,
cut into thin strips

55 g/2 oz rocket

salt and pepper

Method

1 Bring a large saucepan of lightly salted water to the boil. Add the pasta, bring back to the boil and cook for 8–10 minutes, until tender but still firm to the bite.

2 Meanwhile, heat the oil in a large frying pan over a low heat. Add the garlic and cook for 1 minute, stirring constantly.

3 Add the salmon and rocket. Season to taste with pepper and cook, stirring constantly, for 1 minute. Remove the frying pan from the heat.

4 Drain the pasta and combine with the smoked salmon and rocket mixture. Transfer to warmed serving plates and serve immediately.

FISH & SEAFOOD

GRILLED TROUT WITH LEMON PARSLEY SAUCE

Serves: 6   **Prep: 15 mins**   **Cook: 8–10 mins**

Ingredients

6 tbsp unsalted butter, plus extra for greasing

6 whole rainbow trout, butterflied

3 tbsp fresh lemon juice

large handful of chopped fresh parsley

salt and pepper

lemon wedges, to serve

Method

1 Put the butter into a saucepan over a medium–low heat and cook until the butter turns golden brown, and gives off a nutty aroma. Reduce the heat to very low and keep warm. Preheat the grill to medium.

2 Line a large baking sheet with foil and grease. Remove the heads from the fish, butterfly and place, skin-side down, on the prepared baking sheet. Lightly brush a little of the browned butter over the surface of the fish. Season to taste with salt and pepper.

3 Place the fish under the grill about 10 cm/4 inches from the heat and cook for 3–5 minutes, or until the fish flakes when separated gently with a fork.

4 Meanwhile, increase the heat under the butter to medium and whisk in the lemon juice. As soon as the mixture comes to the boil, add the parsley and remove from the heat. Serve the trout on warmed plates with the hot butter spooned over and lemon wedges on the side.

FISH & SEAFOOD

HALIBUT WITH TOMATO & ALMOND SAUCE

Serves: 4

Prep: 15–20 mins, plus cooling

Cook: 16–18 mins

Ingredients

675 g/1 lb 8 oz halibut fillets

¾ tsp salt

½ tsp pepper

green vegetables, to serve

Sauce

1 large red pepper

3 garlic cloves

25 g/1 oz flaked, toasted almonds

1 thick slice of bread, torn into a few pieces

1 tsp salt

1 tsp paprika

250 g/9 oz canned chopped tomatoes

2 tbsp red wine vinegar

Method

1 To make the sauce, preheat the grill. Quarter the pepper and place the pieces, cut-side down, on a baking sheet with the garlic cloves. Grill, turning the garlic once, until the garlic is browned and soft, and the skin of the pepper blackens and blisters. Remove from the grill and set aside to cool slightly.

2 When cool enough to handle, peel the blackened skin from the pepper and remove the core and seeds, discarding both. Put the pepper and garlic in a food processor with the almonds, bread, salt and paprika. Process to a paste. Add the tomatoes and vinegar and process until the tomatoes are smooth and fully incorporated.

3 To cook the fish, preheat a grill to high or heat a griddle pan over a high heat. Season the fish with the salt and pepper and grill for about 4 minutes. Turn and grill on the other side for a further 4 minutes, or until the fish is opaque and cooked through. Serve immediately, with the sauce drizzled over and green vegetables on the side.

SPICED MACKEREL WITH MANGO SALSA

Serves: 4   **Prep: 15–20 mins**   **Cook: 8–10 mins**

Ingredients

2 tsp ground coriander

2 tsp ground cumin

½ tsp ground turmeric

¼ tsp cayenne pepper

pinch of salt

8 mackerel fillets

flatbreads, to serve

Salsa

1 small avocado

1 small mango

1 small onion, finely chopped

juice of 1 lime

Method

1 Preheat a ridged griddle pan. Mix together the coriander, cumin, turmeric, cayenne and salt.

2 Cut deep slashes in the skin side of each mackerel fillet and rub the spices all over.

3 For the salsa, halve, stone and peel the avocado and mango, then cut into fine dice. Mix with the onion and lime juice.

4 Cook the mackerel in the preheated griddle pan for 6–8 minutes, turning once, until cooked through.

5 Serve the mackerel with the salsa spooned over, accompanied by flatbreads.

FISH & SEAFOOD

SEA BASS WITH OLIVE GREMOLATA

Serves: 4   **Prep: 10–15 mins**   **Cook: 15–20 mins**

Ingredients

900 g/2 lb small new potatoes

4 sea bass fillets, about 175 g/6 oz each

1 tbsp olive oil

4 tbsp dry white wine

salt and pepper

lemon wedges, to serve

Olive gremolata

grated rind of 1 lemon

1 garlic clove, chopped

2 large handfuls flat-leaf parsley

70 g/2½ oz stoned black olives

2 tbsp capers

2 tbsp olive oil

Method

1 Cook the potatoes in a saucepan of lightly salted boiling water for 15–20 minutes, or until tender.

2 Meanwhile, make the gremolata. Place the lemon rind, garlic, parsley, olives, capers and oil in a food processor or blender, and process briefly to form a rough paste.

3 Brush the sea bass with the oil and season to taste with salt and pepper. Heat a heavy-based frying pan and fry the sea bass for 5–6 minutes, turning once.

4 Remove the fish from the pan and keep warm. Stir the wine into the pan and boil for 1 minute, stirring. Add the gremolata to the pan and stir for a few seconds to heat gently.

5 Drain the potatoes when tender and crush lightly with a wooden spoon or potato masher.

6 Transfer the sea bass and crushed potatoes to warmed serving plates and serve immediately with the gremolata and lemon wedges.

TURBOT GOUJONS WITH CAPER MAYONNAISE

Serves: 4   **Prep: 20 mins**   **Cook: 18–22 mins**

Ingredients

70 g/2½ oz stale white breadcrumbs

finely grated rind of 1 lemon

2 tbsp finely chopped fresh parsley

500 g/1 lb 2 oz skinless turbot fillet

3 tbsp plain flour

1 egg, beaten

sunflower oil, for frying

salt and pepper

Mayonnaise

4 tbsp mayonnaise

1 tbsp capers, chopped

1 tbsp lemon juice

Method

1 Put the breadcrumbs, lemon rind and parsley into a food processor and process to fine crumbs. Place in a wide dish.

2 Cut the turbot into 7.5- x 2-cm/3- x ¾-inch strips. Season the flour with salt and pepper to taste and place in a wide dish. Put the egg into a separate wide dish.

3 Toss the fish in the seasoned flour to coat evenly, then dip in the beaten egg and, finally, in the breadcrumb mixture, turning to coat completely.

4 To make the caper mayonnaise, mix together all the ingredients in a small bowl. Set aside.

5 Heat enough oil for deep-frying in a large saucepan or deep-fryer to 180–190°C/350–375°F, or until a cube of bread browns in 30 seconds. Add the fish strips in batches and fry, turning once, for 2–3 minutes, until golden. Drain on kitchen paper.

6 Serve the goujons hot, with the caper mayonnaise on the side.

QUICK SEAFOOD BAKE

Serves: 4–6   **Prep: 15–20 mins**   **Cook: 25 mins**

Ingredients

350 g/12 oz new potatoes

4 fresh corn cobs

4 tbsp olive oil

1 tsp salt

60 g/2¼ oz butter, plus extra for greasing

juice of ½ lemon

3 garlic cloves

1 tbsp smoked or sweet paprika

900 g/2 lb live small clams

900 g/2 lb live mussels

350 g/12 oz large raw prawns, peeled and deveined

125 ml/4 fl oz dry white wine

crusty bread, to serve

Dipping sauce

115 g/4 oz butter

3 garlic cloves

Method

1 Preheat the oven to 220°C/425°F/Gas Mark 7 and grease a large baking dish. Slice the potatoes into thin rounds. Break each corn cob into 3–4 pieces. Put the potatoes and corn into the prepared dish. Drizzle with half the oil and half the salt. Cover with foil and bake in the preheated oven for about 20 minutes. Meanwhile, melt the butter in the microwave. Remove and add the remaining oil, the lemon juice, garlic, paprika and the remaining salt.

2 While the vegetables are still cooking, scrub the clams and scrub and debeard the mussels. Discard any clams or mussels with broken shells and any that refuse to close when tapped. Wash the prawns. Remove the foil from the baking dish and add the clams and mussels, nestling them down into the potatoes. Add the wine and replace the foil. Return to the oven and cook for a further 5 minutes.

3 Remove the foil from the baking dish and add the prawns in a layer on top of the vegetables, clams and mussels. Drizzle the butter mixture over the seafood. Replace the foil and return the dish to the oven. Cook for a further 5 minutes, or until the prawns are pink and cooked through and the clams and mussels have opened (discard any clams or mussels that remain closed).

4 Meanwhile, make the dipping sauce. Melt the butter in the microwave. Finely chop the garlic and combine with the butter in a small bowl. Serve the bake with small bowls of sauce and crusty bread for mopping up the juices. Be sure to put out seafood forks, empty bowls for the shells and a finger bowl.

SPICY THAI SEAFOOD STEW

Serves: 4 **Prep: 15–20 mins** **Cook: 10–12 mins**

Ingredients

200 g/7 oz basmati rice

200 g/7 oz squid, cleaned and tentacles discarded

500 g/1 lb 2 oz firm white fish fillets, preferably monkfish or halibut

1 tbsp corn oil

4 shallots, finely chopped

2 garlic cloves, finely chopped

2 tbsp Thai green curry paste

2 small lemon grass stems, finely chopped

1 tsp shrimp paste

500 ml/18 fl oz coconut milk

200 g/7 oz raw king prawns, peeled and deveined

12 live clams, scrubbed

8 fresh basil leaves, finely shredded, plus extra leaves to garnish

salt

Method

1 Cook the rice in a saucepan of lightly salted water for 10–12 minutes, until tender. Drain.

2 Meanwhile, using a sharp knife, cut the squid into thick rings and cut the fish into bite-sized chunks.

3 Preheat a wok or large frying pan over a high heat. Add the oil and heat until very hot. Add the shallots, garlic and curry paste, and stir-fry for 1–2 minutes.

4 Add the lemon grass and shrimp paste, then stir in the coconut milk and bring to the boil.

5 Reduce the heat until the liquid is simmering gently, then add the squid, fish and prawns, and simmer for 2 minutes.

6 Discard any clams with broken shells and any that refuse to close when tapped. Add the clams and simmer for a further minute, or until the clams have opened. Discard any that remain closed. Sprinkle the shredded basil leaves over the stew.

7 Transfer to warmed serving bowls. Garnish with basil leaves and serve immediately with the rice.

PRAWNS WITH SMOKED PAPRIKA

Serves: 2

Prep: 15 mins, plus marinating

Cook: 5–6 mins

Ingredients

450 g/1 lb large raw unpeeled prawns (about 12 prawns)

2 tbsp olive oil

1 tbsp lemon juice

1½ tsp smoked paprika

1 garlic clove, peeled and crushed

sea salt

lemon wedges and crusty bread, to serve

Method

1 Pull the heads off the prawns. Using a sharp knife, cut along the back of each prawn through the shell, and remove and discard the dark vein. Rinse the prawns under cold running water and pat dry with kitchen paper.

2 Mix the olive oil, lemon juice, paprika and garlic together in a large bowl. Add a generous pinch of salt and the prepared prawns. Toss together. Set aside in a cool place for 15–20 minutes to marinate, stirring occasionally.

3 To cook, spread the prawns out in a single layer on a pre-heated smoking-hot ridged grill pan and cook, for 3–4 minutes, turning once, until they turn pink and are just cooked through. Serve immediately with lemon wedges and crusty bread.

CALAMARI WITH PRAWNS & BROAD BEANS

Serves: 6   **Prep: 15 mins**   **Cook: 16–22 mins**

Ingredients

2 tbsp olive oil

4 spring onions, thinly sliced

2 garlic cloves, finely chopped

500 g/1 lb 2 oz squid, cleaned and thickly sliced

100 ml/3½ fl oz dry white wine

225 g/8 oz fresh or frozen baby broad beans

250 g/9 oz raw king prawns, peeled and deveined

4 tbsp chopped fresh flat-leaf parsley

salt and pepper

crusty bread, to serve

Method

1 Heat the oil in a large frying pan over a medium heat. Add the spring onions and cook over a medium heat, stirring occasionally, for 4–5 minutes, until soft.

2 Add the garlic and cook, stirring, for 30 seconds until soft. Add the squid and cook over a high heat, stirring occasionally, for 2 minutes, or until golden brown.

3 Stir in the wine and bring to the boil. Add the beans, reduce the heat, cover and simmer for 5–8 minutes, if using fresh beans, or 4–5 minutes, if using frozen beans, until tender.

4 Add the prawns, re-cover and simmer for a further 2–3 minutes, until the prawns turn pink and start to curl. Stir in the parsley and season to taste with salt and pepper. Transfer to warmed serving bowls and serve immediately with crusty bread.

GINGER PRAWNS WITH OYSTER MUSHROOMS

Serves: 4   **Prep: 15 mins**   **Cook: 12 mins**

Ingredients

3 tbsp vegetable oil

3 carrots, thinly sliced

350 g/12 oz oyster mushrooms, thinly sliced

1 large red pepper, deseeded and thinly sliced

450 g/1 lb raw king prawns, peeled and deveined

2 garlic cloves, crushed

fresh coriander sprigs, to garnish

cooked rice, to serve

Sauce

150 ml/5 fl oz chicken stock

2 tsp sesame seeds

1 tbsp grated fresh ginger

1 tbsp soy sauce

¼ tsp hot pepper sauce

1 tsp cornflour

Method

1 To make the sauce, stir together the stock, sesame seeds, ginger, soy sauce, hot pepper sauce and cornflour until well blended. Set aside.

2 Heat a wok over a medium–high heat, then add 2 tablespoons of oil. Add the carrots and stir-fry for 3 minutes, remove from the wok and set aside.

3 Add the remaining oil to the wok and stir-fry the mushrooms for 2 minutes. Remove from the wok and set aside.

4 Add the red pepper, prawns and garlic to the wok and stir-fry for 3 minutes, until the prawns turn pink and start to curl. Stir the sauce again and pour it into the wok.

5 Cook until the mixture bubbles, then return the carrots and mushrooms to the wok. Cover and cook for a further 2 minutes, until heated through. Serve over freshly cooked rice and garnish with coriander sprigs.

SALT & PEPPER SQUID

Serves: 2   **Prep: 20 mins**   **Cook: 20 mins**

Ingredients

groundnut oil,
for deep-frying

1 large garlic clove,
very thinly sliced

300 g/10½ oz cleaned
squid, sliced into
1-cm/½-inch strips

3 spring onions, green parts
included, sliced diagonally
into 2.5-cm/1-inch lengths

pinch of crushed chilli flakes

2–3 handfuls rocket

Salt and pepper mix

1 tsp Sichuan peppercorns

1 tsp sea salt flakes

Ginger wisps

250 g/9 oz fresh ginger

groundnut oil,
for deep-frying

Method

1 To make the salt and pepper mix, combine the peppercorns and salt. Pound to a coarse powder using a mortar and pestle or a clean electric coffee grinder.

2 To make the ginger wisps, peel the ginger and very thinly slice lengthways. Stack the slices a few at a time, and slice lengthways again into thin matchsticks.

3 Heat enough oil for deep-frying in a large wok to 180–190°C/350–375°F, or until a cube of bread browns in 30 seconds. Add the ginger and fry for 6–7 minutes, until golden and crisp. Remove immediately and drain on kitchen paper. Sprinkle with a little of the salt and pepper mix. Set aside and keep warm.

4 Heat a separate wok over a medium heat. Add the oil and heat until hot, then add the garlic and fry for 30–60 seconds, until pale golden in colour. Remove with a slotted spoon, drain on kitchen paper and set aside.

5 Increase the heat to high and add the squid, spring onions and chilli flakes. Stir-fry for 2 minutes, until the squid is cooked. Arrange the rocket and some ginger wisps on serving plates. Add the squid and sprinkle with the fried garlic and more of the salt and pepper mix. Serve immediately.

FISH & SEAFOOD

BAKED CLAMS WITH BREADCRUMBS

Serves: 4   **Prep: 20–25 mins**   **Cook: 18–20 mins**

Ingredients

85 g/3 oz butter

100 g/3½ oz fresh white breadcrumbs

2 cloves garlic, crushed

3 tbsp fresh snipped chives

600 ml/1 pint boiling water

2 kg/4 lb 8 oz live clams, scrubbed

salt and pepper

chives, to garnish

rocket leaves, to serve

Method

1 Preheat the oven to 220°C/425°F/Gas Mark 7. Melt the butter and stir in the breadcrumbs, garlic and chives. Season with salt and pepper.

2 Discard any clams with broken shells or any that refuse to close when tapped. Bring the water to a fast boil and add the clams, cover and boil for 2–3 minutes, until the clams open. Drain well. Discard any clams that remain closed.

3 Remove the top shells from the clams and arrange the clam-filled shells on a large baking sheet. Place a teaspoonful of the breadcrumb mixture onto each clam.

4 Bake the clams in the oven for 10–12 minutes, or until bubbling and golden brown. Garnish with chives and serve immediately with rocket leaves.

FISH & SEAFOOD

MOULES MARINIÈRES

Serves: 4   **Prep: 20 mins**   **Cook: 8 mins**

Ingredients

2 kg/4 lb 8 oz live mussels

300 ml/10 fl oz dry white wine

6 shallots, finely chopped

1 bouquet garni

pepper

bay leaves, to garnish

fresh crusty bread, to serve

Method

1 Clean and debeard the mussels. Discard any with broken shells and any that refuse to close when tapped. Rinse the mussels thoroughly under cold running water.

2 Pour the wine into a large, heavy-based saucepan, add the shallots and bouquet garni and season to taste with pepper. Bring to the boil over a medium heat. Add the mussels, cover tightly and cook, shaking the saucepan occasionally, for 5 minutes. Remove and discard the bouquet garni and any mussels that remain closed.

3 Divide the mussels between four serving bowls with a slotted spoon. Strain the mussel liquor to remove any remaining grit, then spoon over the mussels, garnish with bay leaves and serve immediately with crusty bread.

PASTA WITH MUSSELS & WHITE WINE

Serves: 4   **Prep: 20 mins**   **Cook: 23–25 mins**

Ingredients

2 kg/4 lb 8 oz mussels, scrubbed and debearded

1 large onion, chopped

3 garlic cloves, finely chopped

500 ml/18 fl oz dry white wine

1 bay leaf

2 sprigs of fresh thyme

5 tbsp chopped fresh flat-leaf parsley

1 tbsp chopped fresh rosemary

4 tbsp butter

450 g/1 lb dried tagliatelle or other broad-ribboned pasta

salt and pepper

Method

1 Rinse and scrub the mussels well, discarding any with broken shells or that refuse to close when tapped.

2 Put the onion, garlic, white wine, herbs and 2 tablespoons of the butter in a saucepan. Bring to the boil, then reduce the heat. Add the mussels, then season to taste with salt and pepper. Cover and cook over a medium heat for 3–4 minutes, shaking the pan, until the mussels open. Remove from the heat. Lift out the mussels with a slotted spoon, reserving the liquid. Discard any that remain closed. Remove most of the mussels from their shells, reserving a few in their shells to garnish. Remove and discard the bay leaf from the liquid. Keep the mussels warm.

3 Bring a large saucepan of lightly salted water to the boil. Add the pasta, bring back to the boil and cook for 8–10 minutes, until tender but still firm to the bite. Drain the pasta and divide between individual warmed serving bowls. Spoon the mussels over the pasta and keep warm. Strain the mussel liquid and return to the pan. Add the remaining butter and heat until melted. Pour over the pasta, garnish with the mussels in their shells and serve immediately.

SEARED SCALLOPS

Serves: 4   **Prep: 15 mins**   **Cook: 8 mins**

Ingredients

3 tbsp olive oil

finely grated rind and juice of 2 limes

2 tbsp chopped fresh coriander

1 garlic clove, finely chopped

pinch of dried crushed chillies (optional)

125 g/4½ oz mixed salad leaves

16 shucked scallops, thawed if frozen

salt and pepper

Method

1 Whisk together the oil, lime rind and juice, coriander, garlic and chillies, if using, in a bowl and season to taste with salt and pepper. Add the salad leaves and toss well, then divide the leaves between four individual serving plates. Reserve the remaining dressing.

2 Heat a ridged griddle pan until very hot. Meanwhile, pat the scallops dry with kitchen paper. Add the scallops to the hot pan and cook for 3 minutes on each side, then remove the pan from the heat.

3 Divide the scallops between the plates, spoon over the remaining dressing and serve immediately.

SPEEDY PAELLA

Serves: 4   **Prep: 15 mins**   **Cook: 20 mins**

Ingredients

2 tbsp olive oil

1 onion, thinly sliced

1 red romano pepper, sliced

100 g/3½ oz chorizo, sliced

200 g/7 oz long-grain rice

850 ml/1½ pints boiling fish stock

pinch of saffron threads

140 g/5 oz frozen peas

200 g/7 oz cooked peeled tiger prawns

salt and pepper

chopped fresh flat-leaf parsley, to garnish

crusty bread, to serve

Method

1 Heat the oil in a large saucepan over a medium heat. Add the onion and red pepper and cook for 2 minutes, stirring constantly. Stir in the chorizo and rice and cook for a further minute.

2 Add the stock and saffron and bring to the boil. Reduce the heat, cover the pan and simmer for 10 minutes, stirring occasionally, until the rice is almost tender.

3 Stir in the peas and prawns and season to taste with salt and pepper, then cover and cook gently for a further 4–5 minutes, until the rice is tender.

4 Transfer to warmed serving plates. Garnish with parsley and serve immediately with crusty bread.

★ Variation

This dish is a Spanish classic, ideal for a summer evening. Add a little shredded roast chicken to the pan with the peas and prawns to make it really traditional.

VEGETARIAN

GRILLED HALLOUMI KEBABS WITH FENNEL & WHITE BEANS

Serves: 4   **Prep: 20 mins**   **Cook: 10–12 mins**

Ingredients

200 g/7 oz vegetarian halloumi cheese

1 garlic clove, crushed

1 fennel bulb, thinly sliced

1 small red onion, thinly sliced

400 g/14 oz canned cannellini beans, drained

1–2 tbsp balsamic vinegar, to serve

Dressing

finely grated rind and juice of 1 lemon

3 tbsp chopped fresh flat-leaf parsley

4 tbsp olive oil

salt and pepper

Method

1 For the dressing, mix together the lemon rind and juice, parsley and oil with salt and pepper to taste.

2 Cut the halloumi into 2-cm/¾-inch cubes, thread onto four pre-soaked wooden skewers and brush with half the dressing.

3 Preheat a ridged grill pan over a high heat. Cook the skewers in the pan, for 6–8 minutes, turning once, until golden.

4 Heat the remaining dressing and the garlic in a small pan until boiling. Combine with the fennel, onion and beans.

5 Serve the skewers with the salad, sprinkled with a little balsamic vinegar.

★ Variation

Halloumi cheese is perfect for cooking with because it holds its shape well, even when heated. Try frying these delicious kebabs on the barbecue for an extra smokey flavour.

VEGETARIAN

PAPPARDELLE WITH CHERRY TOMATOES, ROCKET & MOZZARELLA

Serves: 4   **Prep: 15 mins**   **Cook: 13–15 mins**

Ingredients

400 g/14 oz dried pappardelle

2 tbsp olive oil

1 garlic clove, chopped

350 g/12 oz cherry tomatoes, halved

85 g/3 oz rocket leaves

300 g/10½ oz vegetarian mozzarella, chopped

salt and pepper

grated Parmesan-style vegetarian cheese, to serve

Method

1 Bring a large saucepan of lightly salted water to the boil. Add the pasta, bring back to the boil and cook for 8–10 minutes, until tender but still firm to the bite.

2 Meanwhile, heat the oil in a frying pan over a medium heat and fry the garlic, stirring, for 1 minute, without browning.

3 Add the tomatoes, season well with salt and pepper and cook gently for 2–3 minutes, until softened.

4 Drain the pasta and stir into the frying pan. Add the rocket leaves and mozzarella, then stir until the leaves wilt.

5 Transfer to warmed serving bowls and serve immediately with Parmesan-style cheese.

VEGETARIAN

TAGLIATELLE WITH HAZELNUT PESTO

Serves: 4   **Prep: 15 mins**   **Cook: 13–15 mins**

Ingredients

350 g/12 oz dried tagliatelle

175 g/6 oz fresh or frozen broad beans

Pesto

1 garlic clove, roughly chopped

55 g/2 oz hazelnuts

100 g/3½ oz wild rocket

4 tbsp olive oil

salt and pepper

Method

1 To make the pesto, place the garlic, hazelnuts, rocket and oil in a food processor and process to a rough paste. Season to taste with salt and pepper.

2 Bring a large pan of lightly salted water to the boil. Add the pasta, return to the boil and cook for 8–10 minutes, or until tender but still firm to the bite. Add the broad beans 3–4 minutes before the end of the cooking time.

3 Drain the pasta and beans well, then tip back into the pan. Add the pesto and toss to coat evenly. Serve immediately.

VEGETARIAN

SPEEDY VEGETABLE LASAGNE

Serves: 4   **Prep: 20-25 mins**   **Cook: 8-10 mins**

Ingredients

1 red onion, sliced into wedges

1 green pepper, deseeded and roughly sliced

1 red pepper, deseeded and roughly sliced

2 large courgettes, sliced diagonally

2 tbsp olive oil, plus extra for greasing

12 squares of fresh lasagne (about 10 cm/4 inch wide)

handful of fresh basil leaves

2 large tomatoes, sliced

100 g/3½ oz vegetarian Cheddar cheese, grated

salt and pepper

mixed salad leaves, to serve

Method

1 Preheat the grill to high. Arrange the onion, green pepper, red pepper and courgettes on a baking sheet and drizzle with the oil. Sprinkle with salt and pepper and grill for 6–8 minutes, turning once, until tender.

2 Meanwhile, cook the lasagne in a large saucepan of boiling, salted water for 2–3 minutes, or until tender. Drain well.

3 Place four lasagne sheets on a greased baking sheet. Take half of the vegetable mixture and divide between the four sheets. Top each with basil leaves and tomato slices and top with a lasagne sheet. Divide the remaining vegetable mixture between the four lasagne stacks and then top each with another lasagne sheet.

4 Sprinkle with grated cheese. Cook the lasagne stacks under the preheated grill for 2 minutes, until the cheese is melted and bubbling.

5 Transfer to warmed serving plates and serve immediately with mixed salad leaves.

VEGETARIAN

KALE PESTO & SPAGHETTI

Serves: 4   **Prep: 20 mins**   **Cook: 20 mins**

Ingredients

225 g/8 oz kale

40 g/1½ oz pine nuts

450 g/1 lb dried spaghetti

1 large garlic clove

1 lemon

125 ml/4 fl oz olive oil

30 g/1 oz grated Parmesan-style vegetarian cheese, plus extra to garnish

400 g/14 oz canned cannellini beans

2 tbsp chia seeds, to garnish

salt

Method

1. Bring a large saucepan of lightly salted water to the boil and fill a medium-sized bowl with iced water. Trim the stems and centre ribs from the kale and blanch the leaves in the boiling water for 45 seconds. Using a slotted spoon, transfer the kale to the iced water. Drain the kale, place it in a clean tea towel and squeeze to remove any excess water. Heat a large frying pan over a medium heat, place a layer of baking paper on the base and scatter over the pine nuts. Gently toast until the nuts turn golden. Set aside.

2. Bring the saucepan of salted water back to the boil and add the pasta. Cook for 8–10 minutes, until tender but still firm to the bite. Meanwhile, combine the kale, pine nuts, garlic and ¾ teaspoon of salt in a food processor. Zest the lemon into the bowl of the processor, then halve the lemon and squeeze in the juice of one half. Pulse until smooth. Drizzle in the oil until it is fully incorporated. Add the cheese and pulse to mix.

3. Drain and rinse the beans, then add to the pasta. Immediately drain the pasta, reserving some of the cooking water. Toss the pasta and beans with the pesto. Add a little of the reserved cooking water if needed to coat the pasta nicely. Serve immediately with a generous dusting of cheese and a sprinkling of chia seeds.

VEGETARIAN

PASTA SALAD WITH CHARGRILLED PEPPERS

Serves: 4 **Prep: 20 mins** **Cook: 15 mins**

Ingredients

1 red pepper

1 orange pepper

280 g/10 oz dried conchiglie

5 tbsp extra virgin olive oil

2 tbsp lemon juice

2 tbsp green pesto

1 garlic clove, finely chopped

3 tbsp shredded fresh basil leaves

salt and pepper

Method

1 Preheat the grill. Put the whole peppers on a baking tray and place under the hot grill, turning frequently, for 15 minutes, or until charred all over. Remove with tongs and place in a bowl. Cover with crumpled kitchen paper and set aside.

2 Meanwhile, bring a large saucepan of lightly salted water to the boil. Add the pasta, return to the boil and cook for 8–10 minutes, or until the pasta is tender but still firm to the bite.

3 Combine the oil, lemon juice, pesto and garlic in a large bowl, whisking well to mix. Drain the pasta, add it to the oil mixture while still hot and toss well. Set aside until required.

4 When the peppers are cool enough to handle, peel off the skins, then cut open and remove the seeds. Chop the flesh roughly and add to the pasta with the basil. Season to taste with salt and pepper, and toss well. Serve.

VEGETARIAN

CHEESY SWEETCORN FRITTERS

Serves: 8   **Prep: 15 mins**   **Cook: 3–4 mins**

Ingredients

1 egg

200 ml/7 fl oz milk

100 g/3½ oz plain flour

½ tsp baking powder

85 g/3 oz canned
sweetcorn kernels, drained

4 tbsp grated vegetarian
Cheddar cheese

1 tsp snipped fresh chives

2 tsp sunflower oil

Method

1 Put the egg and milk into a medium bowl and beat with a fork.

2 Add the flour and baking powder, and beat until smooth. Stir in the sweetcorn, cheese and chives.

3 Heat the oil in a non-stick frying pan over a medium heat. Drop tablespoonfuls of the batter into the pan.

4 Cook for 1–2 minutes, until the fritters are puffed up and golden. Flip and cook for a further minute on the opposite side. Remove and drain on kitchen paper, and serve.

VEGETARIAN

POTATO FRITTERS WITH ONION & TOMATO RELISH

Serves: 8 **Prep: 25 mins,** plus standing **Cook: 13-17 mins**

Ingredients

55 g/2 oz wholemeal flour

½ tsp ground coriander

½ tsp cumin seeds

¼ tsp chilli powder

½ tsp turmeric

¼ tsp salt

1 egg

3 tbsp milk

350 g/12 oz potatoes

1–2 garlic cloves, crushed

4 spring onions, chopped

55 g/2 oz sweetcorn kernels

vegetable oil, for shallow-frying

Onion & tomato relish

1 onion

225 g/8 oz tomatoes

2 tbsp chopped fresh coriander

2 tbsp chopped fresh mint

2 tbsp lemon juice

½ tsp roasted cumin seeds

¼ tsp salt

pinch of cayenne pepper

Method

1 First, make the relish. Cut the onion and tomatoes into small dice and place in a bowl with the remaining ingredients. Mix together well and leave to stand for at least 15 minutes before serving to allow the flavours to blend.

2 Place the flour in a bowl, stir in the spices and salt, and make a well in the centre. Add the egg and milk, and mix to form a fairly thick batter.

3 Coarsely grate the potatoes, place them in a sieve and rinse well under cold running water. Drain and squeeze dry, then stir them into the batter with the garlic, spring onions and sweetcorn, and mix to combine thoroughly.

4 Heat about 5 mm/¼ inch of oil in a large frying pan and add a few tablespoons of the mixture at a time, flattening each to form a thin cake. Fry over a low heat, turning frequently, for 2–3 minutes, or until golden brown and cooked through.

5 Drain the fritters on kitchen paper and keep them hot while frying the remaining mixture. Serve the potato fritters hot with the relish.

VEGETARIAN

POTATO & CHIVE PANCAKES

Serves: 4

Prep: 15 mins, plus standing

Cook: 13–17 mins

Ingredients

150 g/5½ oz plain flour

1½ tsp baking powder

250 ml/9 fl oz milk

1 large egg

2 tbsp sunflower oil, plus extra for greasing

225 g/8 oz potatoes

2 tbsp snipped chives

1 tbsp wholegrain mustard

salt and pepper

Greek-style yogurt or soured cream, to serve

Method

1 Sift the flour, baking powder and a pinch of salt into a bowl. Add the milk, egg and oil, and whisk to a smooth batter.

2 Peel the potatoes and grate coarsely, then place in a colander or sieve and sprinkle with salt. Leave to stand for 5 minutes, then press out as much liquid as possible. Stir the grated potato into the batter with the chives, mustard and pepper, to taste.

3 Lightly grease a griddle or frying pan and heat over a medium heat. Spoon tablespoons of batter into the pan and cook until bubbles appear on the surface.

4 Turn over with a palette knife and cook the other side until golden brown. Repeat this process using the remaining batter, while keeping the cooked pancakes warm. Serve immediately with a spoonful of yogurt on the side.

VIETNAMESE VEGETABLE CURRY

Serves: 6   **Prep: 15 mins**   **Cook: 28–30 mins**

Ingredients

2 lemon grass stalks

50 ml/2 fl oz vegetable oil

3 large garlic cloves, crushed

1 large shallot, thinly sliced

2 tbsp Indian curry powder

700 ml/1¼ pints coconut milk

500 ml/18 fl oz coconut water (not coconut milk) or vegetable stock

2 tbsp fish sauce

4 fresh red bird's eye chillies or dried red Chinese chillies

6 kaffir lime leaves

1 carrot, peeled and cut diagonally into 1-cm/½-inch thick pieces

1 small–medium Asian aubergine, cut into 2.5-cm/1-inch pieces

1 small–medium bamboo shoot, cut into thin wedges

115 g/4 oz mangetout, topped and tailed

12 large shiitake mushrooms, stems discarded, caps halved

450 g/1 lb firm tofu, drained and cut into 2.5-cm/1-inch cubes

fresh chopped coriander and fried shallots, to garnish

Method

1 Discard the bruised leaves and root ends of the lemon grass stalks, then cut 15–20 cm/6–8 inches of the lower stalks into paper-thin slices.

2 Heat a wok over a high heat, then add the oil. Add the garlic and shallot, and stir-fry for 5 minutes, or until golden. Add the lemon grass and curry powder and stir-fry for 2 minutes, or until fragrant.

3 Add the coconut milk, coconut water, fish sauce, chillies and lime leaves, and bring to the boil. Reduce the heat to low, then add the carrot and aubergine, cover and cook for 10 minutes.

4 Add the bamboo shoot, mangetout, mushrooms and tofu, and cook for a further 5 minutes.

5 Serve immediately, garnished with the coriander and fried shallots.

VEGETARIAN

RICE & LENTIL CURRY

Serves: 4   **Prep: 15 mins**   **Cook: 23–28 mins**

Ingredients

2.5-cm/1-inch piece fresh ginger

2 garlic cloves

1 onion

2 carrots

225 g/8 oz cauliflower

225 g/8 oz kale

2 tbsp olive oil

2 tbsp curry powder

1 tsp salt

90 g/3¼ oz basmati rice

90 g/3¼ oz small green lentils or red lentils

700 ml/1¼ pints vegetable stock or water

125 ml/4 fl oz coconut milk

1 lime

natural yogurt and sriracha sauce, to serve

Method

1 Peel and finely chop the ginger and garlic. Dice the onion and carrots. Chop the cauliflower into small pieces. Trim the thick stems and centre ribs from the kale leaves and cut the leaves into ribbons.

2 Heat the oil in a large frying pan over a medium–high heat. Add the ginger, garlic and onion and cook, stirring, for about 2 minutes until the onion begins to soften. Stir in the curry powder and salt. Add the vegetables, rice, lentils, stock and coconut milk and bring to the boil.

3 Reduce the heat to low, cover and simmer for 15–20 minutes, until the lentils and rice are tender. Juice the lime and stir in. Serve immediately topped with yogurt and sriracha sauce.

VEGETARIAN

SPICY BEAN CHILLI

Serves: 4

Prep: 15 mins

Cook: 18 mins

Ingredients

2 tbsp olive oil

1 large onion, chopped

1 large green pepper, deseeded and chopped

2 garlic cloves, crushed

2 tsp dried crushed chillies

400 g/14 oz canned chopped plum tomatoes

300 g/10½ oz canned red kidney beans, drained

300 g/10½ oz canned cannellini beans, drained

3 tbsp chopped fresh coriander

salt and pepper

tortilla chips, to serve

Method

1 Heat the oil in a large frying pan over a medium heat. Add the onion and green pepper, and stir-fry for 8 minutes, until softened and lightly browned.

2 Stir in the garlic and chillies, then add the tomatoes and simmer for 2 minutes.

3 Add the beans and coriander, heat until boiling, then simmer for 5 minutes. Season to taste with salt and pepper.

4 Transfer to warmed serving bowls and serve immediately with tortilla chips.

VEGETARIAN

BEAN BURGERS

Serves: 4 **Prep: 20 mins** **Cook: 18–21 mins**

Ingredients

1 tbsp sunflower oil, plus extra for brushing

1 onion, finely chopped

1 garlic clove, finely chopped

1 tsp ground coriander

1 tsp ground cumin

115 g/4 oz white mushrooms, finely chopped

425 g/15 oz canned borlotti or red kidney beans, drained and rinsed

2 tbsp chopped fresh flat-leaf parsley

plain flour, for dusting

salt and pepper

hamburger buns and salad leaves, to serve

Method

1 Heat the oil in a large frying pan over a medium heat. Add the onion and cook, stirring frequently, for 5 minutes, or until softened. Add the garlic, coriander and cumin and cook, stirring, for a further minute. Add the mushrooms and cook, stirring frequently, for 4–5 minutes until all the liquid has evaporated. Set aside. Preheat the grill.

2 Place the beans in a small mixing bowl and mash with a fork. Add the mushroom mixture and parsley. Season to taste with salt and pepper, and mix together.

3 Divide the mixture into four portions, dust with flour and shape each into a ball, then flatten slightly to make a burger shape of your preferred thickness. Brush lightly with oil.

4 Cook the burgers under the preheated grill for 4–5 minutes. Turn the burgers and cook for a further 4–5 minutes, until cooked through.

5 Place the salad leaves on the bottom halves of the buns, top with the burgers and then the lids. Transfer to serving plates and serve immediately.

VEGETARIAN

SMOKY MUSHROOM & CORIANDER BURGERS

Serves: 6 **Prep: 20 mins** **Cook: 13–15 mins**

Ingredients

425 g/15 oz canned red kidney beans,

2 tbsp sunflower or plus extra for brushing

1 onion, finely chopped

115 g/4 oz mushrooms, finely chopped

1 large carrot, coarsely grated

2 tsp smoked paprika

70 g/2½ oz porridge oats

3 tbsp dark soy sauce

2 tbsp tomato purée

30 g/1 oz fresh coriander, including stalks, chopped

3 tbsp plain flour

salt and pepper

soft rolls, salad leaves sliced avocado and tomato salsa, to serve

Method

1 Drain and rinse the kidney beans and place in a large bowl. Mash as thoroughly as you can with a potato masher. Heat the oil in a frying pan, add the onion and fry for 2 minutes until translucent. Add the mushrooms, carrot and paprika and fry for a further 4 minutes, until the vegetables are soft.

2 Add the fried vegetables to the beans with the oats, soy sauce, tomato purée and coriander. Season with salt and pepper and mix well. Divide into six equal portions and shape into burgers, then turn in the flour to coat lightly.

3 Preheat a griddle pan until smoking. Lightly brush the tops of the burgers with oil, then place oiled-side down on the pan. Cook over a medium heat for 2–3 minutes, until lightly charred underneath. Lightly brush the tops with oil, turn and cook for a further 2-3 minutes on the other side. Serve hot in soft rolls with salad leaves, avocado slices and salsa.

VEGETARIAN

FALAFEL PITTA POCKETS

Serves: 4   **Prep: 20 mins**   **Cook: 7 mins**

Ingredients

2 garlic cloves

2 tbsp chopped fresh flat-leaf parsley

1 tsp ground cumin

½ tsp salt

275 g/9¾ oz canned chickpeas, drained and rinsed

2 spring onions, sliced

2 tbsp plain flour

1 tsp baking powder

1 tbsp vegetable oil

To serve

2 wholemeal pitta breads

tzatziki dip, to serve

2 tomatoes, diced

100 g/3½ oz lettuce, shredded

Method

1 To make the falafel patties, chop the garlic in a food processor. Add the parsley, cumin and salt, and process until finely chopped. Add the chickpeas, spring onions, flour and baking powder, and process until the texture resembles coarse breadcrumbs. Form the falafel mixture into eight patties, about 5 mm/¼-inch thick.

2 In a heavy-based frying pan, heat the oil over a medium–high heat. When the oil is hot, add the patties and cook for about 3 minutes, or until browned on the base. Turn over and cook until browned on the other side. Drain on kitchen paper.

3 To serve, stuff two falafel patties into each pitta half, drizzle with some of the tzatziki dip, then add diced tomato and shredded lettuce. Serve immediately.

VEGETARIAN

PUFF-TOPPED VEGETABLE PIE

Serves: 4   **Prep: 15–20 mins**   **Cook: 20 mins**

Ingredients

2 tbsp olive oil

1 leek, thinly sliced

2 carrots, thinly sliced

225 g/8 oz closed cup mushrooms, sliced

100 g/3½ oz fresh or frozen peas

1 tsp dried tarragon

150 ml/5 fl oz boiling vegetable stock

1 sheet ready-rolled puff pastry (½ x 425 g/15 oz pack)

2 tbsp grated Parmesan-style vegetarian cheese

salt and pepper

boiled new potatoes, to serve

Method

1 Preheat the oven to 220°C/425°F/Gas Mark 7 and place a baking sheet on the shelf to heat.

2 Heat the oil in a large frying pan over a high heat. Add the leek and carrots, and cook for 2 minutes, stirring occasionally. Add the mushrooms and cook for a further 2 minutes. Add the peas, tarragon, stock, and salt and pepper to taste. Tip into a 1.5-litre/2¾-pint shallow ovenproof dish.

3 Place the sheet of pastry on top, tucking in any excess around the edges. Make a small slit in the centre, brush lightly with a little water and sprinkle with Parmesan-style cheese.

4 Place the dish on the baking sheet in the preheated oven and bake for 15 minutes, or until golden brown and well risen.

5 Transfer to warmed serving plates and serve immediately with new potatoes.

CELERIAC, CHESTNUT, SPINACH & FETA FILO PIES

Serves: 4   **Prep: 15 mins**   **Cook: 26–30 mins**

Ingredients

4 tbsp olive oil

2 garlic cloves, crushed

½ large or 1 whole small head celeriac, cut into short, thin sticks

250 g/9 oz baby spinach leaves

85 g/3 oz cooked, peeled chestnuts, coarsely chopped

200 g/7 oz vegetarian feta cheese, crumbled

1 egg

2 tbsp pesto sauce

1 tbsp finely chopped fresh parsley

pepper

4 sheets filo pastry (about 32 x 18 cm/13 x 7 inches each)

Method

1 Preheat the oven to 190°C/375°F/Gas Mark 5. Heat 1 tablespoon of the oil in a large frying pan over medium heat, add the garlic and cook for 1 minute, stirring constantly. Add the celeriac and cook for 5 minutes, or until soft and browned. Remove from the pan and keep warm.

2 Add 1 tablespoon of the remaining oil to the frying pan, then add the spinach, cover and cook for 2–3 minutes, or until the spinach has wilted. Uncover and cook until any liquid has evaporated.

3 Mix the garlic and celeriac, spinach, chestnuts, cheese, egg, pesto, parsley and pepper to taste in a large bowl. Divide the mixture between four individual greased gratin dishes or put it all into one medium gratin dish.

4 Brush each sheet of filo with the remaining oil and arrange, slightly scrunched, on top of the celeriac mixture. Bake in the preheated oven, for 15–20 minutes, or until browned. Serve immediately.

VEGETARIAN

SPICY POLENTA WITH POACHED EGGS

Serves: 4

Prep: 20 mins,
plus cooling

Cook: 15–18 mins

Ingredients

oil, for oiling

600 ml/1 pint water

150 g/5½ oz polenta

85 g/3 oz freshly grated
Parmesan-style vegetarian
cheese

40 g/1½ oz butter

½–1 red chilli, deseeded
and very finely chopped

200 g/7 oz baby spinach
leaves, or a mixture of baby
spinach leaves and rocket
leaves

2 tsp white wine vinegar

4 large eggs

salt and pepper

Method

1 Lightly oil an 18-cm/7-inch square cake tin. Bring the water to the boil in a saucepan. Add the polenta in a thin stream and cook, stirring, over a medium–low heat for 3 minutes, until thick. Stir in 55 g/2 oz of the cheese, 30 g/1 oz of the butter and the chilli. Working quickly, transfer to the prepared tin and level the surface. Set aside for 30 minutes until cool and firm, then cut out four rounds with a 9-cm/3½-inch cutter and transfer to a baking tray. Preheat the grill to high.

2 Wash the spinach and place in a large saucepan with the water clinging to the leaves. Cover and cook for 2–3 minutes until wilted, then squeeze with your hands to remove any excess water. Return to the pan.

3 Sprinkle the polenta rounds with the remaining cheese, place under the preheated grill and cook for 3 minutes, until brown and bubbling on the top. Keep warm. Meanwhile, add the remaining butter and salt and pepper to taste to the spinach, and heat through.

4 Half-fill a saucepan with water, add the vinegar and bring to simmering point. Crack the eggs into cups and slide gently into the water. Cook over a low heat, without allowing the water to boil, for 3 minutes until the whites are firm and

VEGETARIAN

boil, for 3 minutes until the whites are firm and the yolk is still soft. Scoop out with a slotted spoon and drain briefly on kitchen paper.

5 To serve, place the polenta rounds on four warmed plates and divide the spinach between them. Top with the eggs and sprinkle with a little salt and pepper. Serve immediately.

GRILLED VEGETABLE SUBS WITH SALAD

Serves: 4   **Prep: 20 mins**   **Cook: 12 mins**

Ingredients

1 small aubergine

2 garlic cloves

2 tbsp olive oil

2 red, yellow or green peppers

1 courgette

1 red onion

4 submarine rolls

4 tbsp pesto

salt and pepper

Salad

280 g/10 oz washed mixed salad leaves

3 tbsp red wine vinegar

½ tsp salt

¼ tsp pepper

4 tbsp olive oil

55 g/2 oz Parmesan-style vegetarian cheese

Method

1 Line a large plate with a double layer of kitchen paper. Slice the aubergine into 5-mm/¼-inch thick rounds and sprinkle with salt. Lay in a single layer on the prepared plate. Finely chop the garlic, put in a small bowl with the oil and mix to combine. Core the peppers and slice into rings. Slice the courgette lengthways into 5-mm/¼-inch wide strips. Slice the onion into 5-mm/¼-inch wide rings. Blot the aubergine dry with kitchen paper, then brush all the vegetables on both sides with the garlic oil and sprinkle with salt and pepper.

2 Heat a ridged grill pan over a high heat and add the vegetables in a single layer. Cook for about 4 minutes on each side, until soft and tender and ridge marks appear. Meanwhile, split the rolls and spread the inside of each with some pesto. To make the salad, put the salad leaves into a bowl. Put the vinegar, salt and pepper into a small bowl, then slowly whisk in the oil. Toss the dressing with the salad leaves. Shave the cheese over the salad and lightly toss again.

VEGETARIAN

3 Pile the vegetables onto the bottom half of each roll in layers and top with the cheese. Put the rolls back onto the grill pan, place under a hot grill, cheese-side up, and cook for about 2 minutes, until the cheese begins to melt. Add the top of the roll and serve hot with the salad.

VEGETABLE STEW WITH COUSCOUS

Serves: 4   **Prep: 15 mins**   **Cook: 15 mins,**
plus standing

Ingredients

1 onion

2 garlic cloves

2 tbsp olive oil

1 orange or red pepper

225 g/8 oz French beans

400 g/14 oz canned
chickpeas

2 tbsp garam masala

1 tsp salt

225 ml/8 fl oz vegetable
stock

400 g/14 oz canned
chopped tomatoes with
their can juices

200 g/7 oz couscous

300 g/10½ oz washed baby
spinach

2 tbsp chopped fresh
parsley

1 lemon

To garnish

natural yogurt

sriracha sauce

chia seeds

Method

1 Dice the onion and finely chop the garlic. Heat the oil in a large frying pan over a medium–high heat. Add the onion and garlic and cook, stirring occasionally, for about 5 minutes, until the onion is soft. Meanwhile, deseed and dice the orange pepper. Top and tail the beans and cut them into 5-cm/2-inch pieces. Drain and rinse the chickpeas.

2 Add the beans and orange pepper to the pan with the chickpeas, garam masala and salt. Add the stock and the tomatoes with their can juices and bring to the boil. Cook for about 4 minutes until the beans begin to soften. Stir in the couscous and spinach, remove from the heat and cover. Leave to stand for about 5 minutes, until the couscous is tender and the spinach is wilted. Meanwhile, finely chop the parsley.

3 Juice the lemon and stir into the stew with the parsley. Serve hot, garnished with a dollop of yogurt, a drizzle of sriracha sauce and a sprinkling of chia seeds.

VEGETARIAN

ASPARAGUS & SUN-DRIED TOMATO RISOTTO

Serves: 4　　　　**Prep: 10 mins**　　　　**Cook: 35 mins**

Ingredients

1 litre/1¾ pints vegetable stock

1 tbsp olive oil

40 g/1½ oz butter

1 small onion, finely chopped

6 sun-dried tomatoes, thinly sliced

280 g/10 oz risotto rice

150 ml/5 fl oz dry white wine

225 g/8 oz fresh asparagus spears, cooked

85 g/3 oz Parmesan-style vegetarian cheese, grated, plus extra to garnish

salt and pepper

grated lemon rind, to garnish

Method

1 Bring the stock to the boil in a saucepan, then reduce the heat and keep simmering gently over a low heat while you are cooking the risotto.

2 Heat the oil with 25 g/1 oz of the butter in a deep saucepan over a medium heat until the butter has melted.

3 Stir in the onion and sun-dried tomatoes and cook, stirring occasionally, for 5 minutes, until the onion is soft and starting to turn golden. Do not brown.

4 Reduce the heat, add the rice and mix to coat in oil and butter. Cook, stirring constantly, for 2–3 minutes, or until the grains are translucent. Add the wine and cook, stirring constantly, until it has reduced.

5 Gradually add the hot stock, a ladleful at a time. Stir constantly and add more liquid as the rice absorbs each addition. Increase the heat to medium so that the liquid bubbles. Cook for 20 minutes, or until all the liquid is absorbed and the rice is creamy but still firm to the bite.

6 While the risotto is cooking, cut most of the asparagus into pieces about 2.5 cm/1 inch long. Set aside several asparagus tips for garnishing the finished dish. Carefully fold the remaining

VEGETARIAN

asparagus into the risotto for the last 5 minutes of cooking time.

7 Remove the risotto from the heat and add the remaining butter. Mix well, then stir in the Parmesan cheese until it melts. Season to taste with salt and pepper. Spoon the risotto into individual warmed serving dishes and garnish with reserved asparagus tips. Sprinkle some Parmesan cheese and lemon rind on top and serve.

RISOTTO WITH PEAS & GORGONZOLA

Serves: 4   **Prep: 15 mins**   **Cook: 28–30 mins**

Ingredients

2 tbsp olive oil

25 g/1 oz butter

1 onion, finely chopped

1 garlic clove, finely chopped

350 g/12 oz risotto rice

150 ml/5 fl oz dry white wine

1.3 litres/2¼ pints hot vegetable stock

350 g/12 oz frozen peas

150 g/5½ oz vegetarian Gorgonzola cheese, crumbled

2 tbsp chopped fresh mint

salt and pepper

Method

1 Heat the oil and butter in a large saucepan over a medium heat. Add the onion and cook, stirring frequently, for 3–4 minutes, until softened.

2 Add the garlic and rice and mix to coat in the butter and oil. Cook, stirring constantly, for 2–3 minutes, or until the grains are translucent. Add the wine and cook, stirring constantly, for 1 minute, until reduced.

3 Gradually add the hot stock, a ladleful at a time. Cook, stirring, for 15 minutes, then stir in the peas and cook for a further 5 minutes, until the liquid is absorbed and the rice is creamy.

4 Remove from the heat. Stir in the Gorgonzola and mint, then season to taste with salt and pepper.

5 Transfer to warmed serving bowls and serve immediately.

VEGETARIAN

MIXED MUSHROOM PIZZA

Serves: 2　　　　**Prep: 20 mins**　　　　**Cook: 16–19 mins**

Ingredients

3 tbsp olive oil

2 garlic cloves, crushed

2 tbsp chopped fresh oregano

2 x 23-cm/9-inch ready-made thin-and-crispy pizza bases

85 g/3 oz vegetarian ricotta cheese

1 tbsp milk

40 g/1½ oz butter

350 g/12 oz mixed mushrooms, sliced

2 tsp lemon juice

1 tbsp chopped fresh marjoram

4 tbsp grated Parmesan-style vegetarian cheese

salt and pepper

Method

1 Preheat the oven to 240°C/475°F/Gas Mark 9. Mix 2 tablespoons of the oil, the garlic and oregano together, and brush over the pizza bases.

2 Mix the ricotta cheese and milk together in a bowl. Season to taste with salt and pepper, and spread the mixture over the pizza bases, leaving a 4-cm/1½-inch border around the edges.

3 Heat the butter and the remaining oil together in a large frying pan. Add the mushrooms and cook over a high heat for 2 minutes. Remove the frying pan from the heat, season to taste with salt and pepper, and stir in the lemon juice and marjoram.

4 Spoon the mushroom mixture over the pizza bases, leaving a 1-cm/½-inch border. Sprinkle with the Parmesan cheese, then bake in the preheated oven for 12–15 minutes, until the crusts are crisp and the mushrooms are cooked. Serve immediately.

VEGETARIAN

CHEESY BAKED COURGETTES

Serves: 4　　　**Prep: 15–20 mins**　　　**Cook: 15 mins**

Ingredients

4 medium courgettes

2 tbsp extra virgin olive oil

115 g/4 oz vegetarian mozzarella cheese, sliced thinly

2 large tomatoes, deseeded and diced

2 tsp chopped fresh basil or oregano

Method

1 Preheat the oven to 200°C/400°F/Gas Mark 6. Slice each courgette lengthways into four strips, keeping the stem ends intact to hold them together. Spread the slices into a fan shape. Brush with oil and place on a large baking sheet.

2 Bake the courgettes in the preheated oven for 10 minutes, without letting them get too soft.

3 Remove the courgettes from the oven. Arrange slices of cheese on top and sprinkle with diced tomatoes and basil. Return to the oven for 5 minutes, or until the cheese has melted and starting to turn golden.

4 Transfer to warmed serving plates and serve immediately.

VEGETARIAN

AUBERGINE GRATIN

Serves: 2   **Prep: 10 mins**   **Cook: 30–35 mins**

Ingredients

4 tbsp olive oil

2 onions, finely chopped

2 garlic cloves, very finely chopped

2 aubergines, thickly sliced

3 tbsp chopped fresh flat-leaf parsley, plus extra sprigs to garnish

½ tsp dried thyme

400 g/14 oz canned chopped tomatoes

175 g/6 oz vegetarian mozzarella cheese, coarsely grated

6 tbsp freshly grated Parmesan-style vegetarian cheese

salt and pepper

Method

1 Preheat the oven to 200°C/400°F/Gas Mark 6. Heat the oil in a flameproof casserole over a medium heat. Add the onions and cook for 5 minutes, or until soft.

2 Add the garlic and cook for a few seconds, or until just beginning to colour. Using a slotted spoon, transfer the onion mixture to a plate.

3 Add the aubergine slices to the casserole in batches and cook until lightly browned. Transfer to another plate.

4 Arrange a layer of aubergine slices in the base of the casserole or a shallow ovenproof dish. Sprinkle with some of the parsley, thyme, and salt and pepper to taste.

5 Add layers of onion, tomatoes and mozzarella, sprinkling parsley, thyme, and salt and pepper to taste over each layer. Continue layering, finishing with a layer of aubergine slices.

6 Sprinkle with the Parmesan-style cheese and bake, uncovered, in the preheated oven for 20–30 minutes, or until the top is golden and the aubergines are tender. Serve hot, garnished with parsley sprigs.

VEGETARIAN

SWEET & SOUR TOFU WITH VEGETABLES

Serves: 4   **Prep: 15 mins**   **Cook: 10–12 mins**

Ingredients

2 tbsp vegetable oil

2 garlic cloves, crushed

2 celery stalks, thinly sliced

1 carrot, cut into thin strips

1 green pepper, diced

85 g/3 oz mangetout,
cut in half diagonally

8 baby sweetcorn

115 g/4 oz beansprouts

450 g/1 lb firm tofu, rinsed,
drained and cut into cubes

Sauce

2 tbsp light brown sugar

2 tbsp wine vinegar

225 ml/8 fl oz vegetable
stock

1 tsp tomato purée

1 tbsp cornflour

Method

1 Preheat a wok or large frying pan over a high heat. Add the oil and heat until very hot. Add the garlic, celery, carrot, pepper, mangetout and baby sweetcorn, and stir-fry for 3–4 minutes.

2 Add the beansprouts and tofu to the wok and cook for 2 minutes, stirring frequently.

3 To make the sauce, place the sugar, wine vinegar, stock, tomato purée and cornflour in a large bowl. Mix together. Stir into the wok, bring to the boil and cook, stirring constantly, until the sauce thickens. Continue to cook for 1 minute.

4 Transfer to warmed serving bowls and serve immediately.

VEGETARIAN

CABBAGE & WALNUT STIR-FRY

Serves: 4   **Prep: 15 mins**   **Cook: 12–13 mins**

Ingredients

4 tbsp groundnut oil

1 tbsp walnut oil

2 garlic cloves, crushed

350 g/12 oz white cabbage, thinly shredded

350 g/12 oz red cabbage, thinly shredded

8 spring onions, trimmed

225 g/8 oz firm tofu, cubed

2 tbsp lemon juice

100 g/3½ oz walnut halves

2 tsp Dijon mustard

salt and pepper

2 tsp poppy seeds, to garnish

Method

1 Preheat a wok or large frying pan over a high heat. Add the oils and heat until very hot. Add the the garlic, white and red cabbage, spring onions and tofu, and cook for 5 minutes, stirring.

2 Add the lemon juice, walnuts and mustard to the wok, and stir to combine thoroughly.

3 Season the mixture to taste with salt and pepper and cook for a further 5 minutes, or until the cabbage is tender.

4 Transfer to warmed serving bowls. Garnish with poppy seeds and serve immediately.

VEGETARIAN

FETA & OLIVE SCONES

Serves: 8　　　**Prep: 20 mins**　　　**Cook: 12–15 mins**

Ingredients

400 g/14 oz self-raising flour

¼ tsp salt

85 g/3 oz butter, plus extra for greasing

40 g/1½ oz pitted black olives, chopped

40 g/1½ oz sun-dried tomatoes in oil, drained and chopped

85 g/3 oz vegetarian feta cheese, crumbled

200 ml/7 fl oz milk, plus extra for glazing

pepper

Method

1 Preheat the oven to 220°C/425°F/Gas Mark 7. Grease a baking sheet.

2 Sift the flour and salt and pepper to taste, into a bowl and rub in the butter evenly with your fingertips.

3 Stir in the olives, tomatoes and feta, then stir in just enough milk to make a soft, smooth dough.

4 Roll out on a floured surface to a 3-cm/1¼-inch thick rectangle. Cut into 6-cm/2½-inch squares. Place on the baking sheet, brush with milk and bake in the preheated oven for 12–15 minutes, until golden.

5 Serve the scones fresh and warm, with extra butter if needed.

★ Variation

Just about any combination of Mediterranean flavours would work well in these scones. Try sun-dried tomatoes and fennel seeds, or garlic and rosemary for other tasty combinations.

VEGETARIAN

BAKING & DESSERTS

HOT CHOCOLATE FUDGE LAYER CAKE

Serves: 8

Prep: 20–25 mins, plus cooling

Cook: 8–10 mins

Ingredients

butter, for greasing

3 eggs

85 g/3 oz caster sugar, plus extra for dusting

85 g/3 oz plain flour

2 tbsp cocoa powder, plus extra for dusting

200 ml/7 fl oz double cream

225 g/8 oz ready-made chocolate fudge frosting

plain and white chocolate curls, to decorate

Method

1 Preheat the oven to 200°C/400°F/Gas Mark 6. Lightly grease a 23 x 33-cm/9 x 13-inch Swiss roll tin and line the base and sides with baking paper. Put the eggs and sugar into a large bowl set over a saucepan of gently simmering water. Whisk with a hand-held electric mixer for 3–4 minutes, or until the mixture is very thick and pale.

2 Sift in the flour and cocoa powder and gently fold in. Pour into the prepared tin and level the surface. Bake in the preheated oven for 8–10 minutes, or until risen and springy to the touch. Meanwhile, dust a sheet of baking paper with caster sugar and whip the cream until it holds firm peaks.

3 Remove the cake from the oven and immediately turn out onto the prepared baking paper. Cut the cake into three strips horizontally and transfer to a wire rack to cool for 5–8 minutes. Spread the frosting over the top of each strip and sandwich the strips together with the cream. Decorate with the chocolate curls and a dusting of cocoa powder.

Nothing goes better with chocolate than coffee and you can give this beautifully moist cake a mocha-flavoured twist by adding a shot of espresso to the chocolate fudge frosting before spreading over the cake.

SUMMER BERRY TARTS

Serves: 6

Prep: 20–25 mins, plus cooling

Cook: 15 mins

Ingredients

375 g/13 oz ready-rolled sweet shortcrust pastry

250 g/9 oz mascarpone cheese

1 tsp vanilla extract

1 tbsp clear honey

400 g/14 oz mixed summer berries, such as strawberries, raspberries, redcurrants and blueberries

icing sugar, for dusting

Method

1 Preheat the oven to 200°C/400°F/Gas Mark 6. Unroll the pastry onto a worktop and cut into six squares. Place each pastry square in a 10-cm/4-inch loose-based tartlet tin and ease lightly into the tin, without stretching.

2 Roll a rolling pin over the top of the tins to trim the excess pastry. Press the pastry into the fluted sides with your fingers.

3 Place the tins on a baking sheet and prick the pastry bases with a fork. Press baking paper into each pastry-lined tin and add baking beans.

4 Bake in the preheated oven for 10 minutes, remove the paper and beans and bake for a further 5 minutes. Leave to cool in the tins for 10 minutes. Carefully remove the tart cases from the tins and leave to cool completely on a wire rack.

5 Mix the mascarpone cheese with the vanilla extract and honey, then spoon into the tartlets and spread evenly.

6 Halve the strawberries and mix with the remaining fruit, then divide between the tartlets. Dust the tartlets with sifted icing sugar just before serving.

APPLE TURNOVERS

Makes: 8   **Prep: 25 mins**   **Cook: 15–20 mins**

Ingredients

250 g/9 oz ready-made puff pastry, thawed, if frozen

flour, for dusting

milk, for glazing

Filling

450 g/1 lb cooking apples, peeled, cored and chopped

grated rind of 1 lemon

pinch of ground cloves

3 tbsp sugar

Orange sugar

1 tbsp sugar, for sprinkling

finely grated rind of 1 orange

Orange cream

250 ml/9 fl oz double cream

grated rind of 1 orange and juice of ½ orange

icing sugar, to taste

Method

1 To make the filling, mix together the apples, lemon rind and ground cloves, but do not add the sugar yet as the juice will seep out of the apples. For the orange sugar, mix together the sugar and orange rind.

2 Preheat the oven to 220°C/425°F/Gas Mark 7. Roll out the pastry on a floured work surface into a 60 x 30-cm/24 x 12-inch rectangle. Cut the pastry in half lengthways, then across into four to make eight 15-cm/6-inch squares.

3 Mix the sugar into the apple filling. Brush each square lightly with milk and place a little of the apple filling in the centre. Fold over one corner diagonally to meet the opposite one, making a triangular turnover, and press the edges together very firmly. Place on a baking sheet. Repeat with the remaining squares. Brush with milk and sprinkle with the orange sugar. Bake in the preheated oven for 15–20 minutes, or until browned. Leave to cool on a wire rack.

4 For the orange cream, whip the cream, orange rind and orange juice together until thick. Add a little icing sugar to taste and whip again until it just holds soft peaks. Serve the turnovers warm with orange cream.

BLUEBERRY & LEMON FRIANDS

Makes: 8

Prep: 20 mins, plus cooling

Cook: 18–22 mins

Ingredients

115 g/4 oz unsalted butter, diced, plus extra for greasing

3 large egg whites

pinch of salt

55 g/2 oz plain flour

150 g/5½ oz icing sugar, plus extra for dusting

85 g/3 oz ground almonds

1 tsp finely grated lemon rind

55 g/2 oz blueberries

Method

1 Preheat the oven to 220°C/425°F/Gas Mark 7. Put the butter into a saucepan and melt over a low heat. Pour into a shallow bowl and leave to cool for a few minutes. Thoroughly grease an 8-hole silicone friand mould or eight holes of a non-stick muffin tin, then place on a baking sheet.

2 Put the egg whites and salt into a large, grease-free bowl and beat with a hand-held electric mixer for 1–2 minutes, until foaming and floppy, but not stiff. Sift in the flour and icing sugar and fold into the egg whites with the ground almonds and lemon rind. Fold in the melted butter to make a smooth batter.

3 Spoon the batter evenly into the prepared mould and scatter over the blueberries. Bake in the preheated oven for 14–18 minutes, until risen, golden and just firm to the touch. Leave to cool in the mould for 5 minutes, then turn out onto a wire rack to cool completely. Serve warm or cold dusted with icing sugar.

GIANT CHOCOLATE CHUNK COOKIES

Makes: 12

Prep: 20 mins,
plus cooling

Cook: 15–20 mins

Ingredients

115 g/4 oz butter, softened

125 g/4½ oz caster sugar

125 g/4½ oz soft light brown sugar

2 large eggs, lightly beaten

1 tsp vanilla extract

280 g/10 oz plain flour

1 tsp bicarbonate of soda

300 g/10½ oz milk chocolate, broken into pieces

Method

1 Preheat the oven to 180°C/350°F/Gas Mark 4. Line four large baking sheets with baking paper.

2 Place the butter and sugars in a large bowl and whisk together until pale and creamy. Whisk the eggs and vanilla extract into the mixture until smooth. Stir in the flour and bicarbonate of soda, and beat together until well mixed. Stir in the chocolate chunks.

3 Drop twelve large spoonfuls of the mixture onto the prepared baking sheets, spacing them well apart. Bake in the preheated oven for 15–20 minutes, or until set and golden brown. Leave to cool on the baking sheets for 2 minutes, then transfer the cookies to wire racks and leave to cool.

WHITE CHOCOLATE & RASPBERRY MUFFINS

Makes: 12

Prep: 20 mins, plus cooling

Cook: 20–25 mins

Ingredients

250 g/9 oz plain flour

1 tbsp baking powder

115 g/4 oz caster sugar

85 g/3 oz butter, chilled and roughly grated

1 large egg, beaten

175 ml/6 fl oz milk

175 g/6 oz raspberries

140 g/5 oz white chocolate chips

Method

1 Preheat the oven to 200°C/400°F/Gas Mark 6. Place 12 paper cases in a muffin tin.

2 Sift together the flour and baking powder into a large bowl and stir in the sugar. Add the butter and stir with a fork to coat in the flour mixture. Lightly beat the egg in a jug or bowl, then beat in the milk.

3 Make a well in the centre of the dry ingredients and pour in the beaten liquid ingredients. Stir gently until just combined; do not over-mix. Fold in the raspberries and half of the chocolate chips.

4 Divide the mixture evenly between the paper cases and scatter over the remaining chocolate chips. Bake in the preheated oven for 20–25 minutes, or until risen, golden and just firm to the touch. Leave to cool for 5 minutes, then transfer to a wire rack to cool completely.

FRUITY FLAPJACKS

Makes: 14

Prep: 15 mins, plus cooling

Cook: 20–25 mins

Ingredients

140 g/5 oz rolled oats

115 g/4 oz demerara sugar

85 g/3 oz raisins

115 g/4 oz butter, melted, plus extra for greasing

Method

1 Preheat the oven to 190°C/375°F/Gas Mark 5. Grease a 28 x 18-cm/11 x 7-inch shallow, rectangular baking tin.

2 Combine the oats, sugar and raisins with the butter, stirring well. Spoon the mixture into the prepared tin and press down firmly with the back of a spoon. Bake in the preheated oven for 15–20 minutes, or until golden.

3 Using a sharp knife, mark into 14 bars, then leave to cool in the tin for 10 minutes. Carefully transfer the bars to a wire rack to cool completely. Once cool, cut into 14 bars to serve.

BAKING & DESSERTS

SUGAR & SPICE DOUGHNUTS

Makes: 6 or 12

Prep: 20 mins, plus cooling

Cook: 15 mins

Ingredients

115 g/4 oz self-raising flour

½ tsp baking powder

70 g/2½ oz caster sugar

1 tsp ground mixed spice

75 ml/2½ fl oz milk

1 egg, beaten

½ tsp vanilla extract

25 g/1 oz butter, melted, plus extra for greasing

Sugar coating

2 tbsp caster sugar

1 tsp ground mixed spice

Method

1 Preheat the oven to 190°C/375°F/Gas Mark 5. Thoroughly grease a 6-hole doughnut tin or a 12-hole mini muffin tin. Sift together the flour and baking powder into a bowl and stir in the sugar and spice. Make a well in the centre. Mix together the milk, egg, vanilla extract and melted butter, and pour into the well. Mix with a wooden spoon until smooth.

2 Spoon the mixture into a piping bag fitted with a plain nozzle (twist the bag around the nozzle before filling to prevent the mixture leaking out, then untwist when ready to pipe). Pipe the mixture as neatly as possible into the prepared tin. Each hole should be about two-thirds full.

3 Bake in the preheated oven for 12–14 minutes, or until risen, golden and firm to the touch. To make the sugar coating, mix together the sugar and mixed spice on a plate. Leave the doughnuts to cool in the tin for 2–3 minutes, then gently ease them out. Toss them in the spiced sugar to coat completely and serve warm or cold.

APPLE STREUSEL CUPCAKES

Makes: 14

Prep: 25 mins, plus cooling

Cook: 20 mins

Ingredients

½ tsp bicarbonate of soda
280 g/10 oz apple sauce
55 g/2 oz butter, softened
85 g/3 oz demerara sugar
1 large egg
175 g/6 oz self-raising flour
½ tsp ground cinnamon
½ tsp freshly grated nutmeg

Topping

50 g/1¾ oz plain flour
50 g/1¾ oz demerara sugar
¼ tsp ground cinnamon
freshly grated nutmeg, to taste
35 g/1¼ oz butter

Method

1 Preheat the oven to 180°C/350°F/Gas Mark 4. Put 14 paper cases in muffin tins.

2 To make the topping, put the flour, demerara sugar, cinnamon and nutmeg in a bowl. Cut the butter into small pieces, then add to the bowl and rub it in with your fingertips until the mixture resembles fine breadcrumbs. Set aside.

3 Add the bicarbonate of soda to the apple sauce and stir until dissolved.

4 Place the butter and demerara sugar in a large bowl and beat together until light and fluffy. Lightly beat the egg in a separate bowl, then add to the butter mixture. Sift in the flour, cinnamon and nutmeg, and fold into the mixture, adding the apple sauce a spoonful at a time.

5 Spoon the mixture into the paper cases. Scatter the topping over the cupcakes and press down gently. Bake in the preheated oven for 20 minutes, or until risen, golden and firm to the touch. Transfer to a wire rack and leave to cool.

LEMON DRIZZLE SQUARES

Makes: 9

Prep: 20 mins, plus cooling

Cook: 20–25 mins

Ingredients

115 g/4 oz butter, softened, plus extra for greasing

115 g/4 oz caster sugar

115 g/4 oz self-raising flour

2 eggs

finely grated rind and juice of ½ large lemon

Topping

85 g/3 oz granulated sugar

finely grated rind and juice of ½ large lemon

Method

1 Preheat the oven to 200°C/400°F/Gas Mark 6. Lightly grease a 20-cm/8-inch shallow square cake tin and line the base and sides with baking paper. Put the butter, sugar, flour, eggs, lemon rind and juice into a large bowl, and beat with an electric hand-held mixer, for 1–2 minutes, until pale and creamy.

2 Spoon the mixture into the prepared tin and gently level the surface. Bake in the preheated oven for 20–25 minutes, or until risen, golden and just firm to the touch. Meanwhile, prepare the topping by mixing together the sugar and lemon rind and juice in a small bowl.

3 Remove the cake from the oven and pierce the top all over with a cocktail stick. Spoon the topping over the hot cake. Leave the cake to cool in the tin – the topping will become crunchy as the cake cools. Remove from the tin and cut into squares to serve.

RASPBERRY & ALMOND CAKE

Serves: 8

Prep: 20 mins,
plus cooling

Cook: 22–25 mins

Ingredients

115 g/4 oz self-raising flour

¼ tsp baking powder

2 eggs

115 g/4 oz butter, softened,
plus extra for greasing

115 g/4 oz caster sugar

40 g/1½ oz ground almonds

175 g/6 oz raspberries

2 tbsp flaked almonds

icing sugar, for dusting

Method

1 Preheat the oven to 200°C/400°F/Gas Mark 6. Place a baking sheet in the oven to heat up. Grease a 23-cm/9-inch round, shallow cake tin and line the base with baking paper. Sift together the flour and baking powder into a large bowl. Add the eggs, butter and sugar, and beat with a hand-held electric mixer for 1–2 minutes, until pale and creamy. Fold in the ground almonds.

2 Spoon the mixture into the prepared tin. Gently level the surface and scatter over the raspberries and flaked almonds. Bake in the preheated oven for 22–25 minutes, or until risen, golden and firm to the touch.

3 Leave the cake to cool in the tin for 1–2 minutes, then turn out onto a wire rack. Serve warm or cold, dusted with icing sugar.

MINI CHOCOLATE WHOOPIE PIES

Makes: 22

Prep: 25 mins, plus cooling

Cook: 7–8 mins

Ingredients

100 g/3½ oz butter, softened

125 g/4½ oz dark muscovado sugar

1 egg, lightly beaten

½ tsp vanilla extract

175 g/6 oz self-raising flour

25 g/1 oz cocoa powder

5 tbsp milk

4–5 tbsp chocolate and hazelnut spread

Method

1 Preheat the oven to 190°C/375°F/Gas Mark 5. Line two large baking sheets with baking paper. Put the butter and sugar into a large bowl and beat with a hand-held electric mixer for 1–2 minutes. Whisk in the egg and vanilla extract. Sift in the flour and cocoa powder, add the milk and fold in gently until thoroughly combined.

2 Pipe or spoon 44 small mounds of the mixture onto the prepared baking sheets. Each mound should be about 4 cm/1½ inches in diameter. Bake in the preheated oven for 7–8 minutes, or until just firm. Carefully transfer the hot cakes to wire racks using a palette knife. Leave to cool for 10 minutes.

3 Sandwich the cakes together with the chocolate and hazelnut spread. If the spread starts to soften because the cakes are still slightly warm, put the filled whoopie pies in the refrigerator for a few minutes until completely cold.

BAKING & DESSERTS

CINNAMON & RAISIN SPIRALS

Makes: 12   **Prep: 20 mins**   **Cook: 14–17 mins**

Ingredients

1 x 325-g/11½-oz sheet ready-rolled puff pastry

25 g/1 oz butter, softened

2 tbsp caster sugar

1 tsp ground cinnamon

55 g/2 oz raisins

2 tbsp apricot jam

Method

1 Preheat the oven to 220°C/425°F/Gas Mark 7. Dampen two baking sheets with a sprinkling of cold water. Unroll the pastry and spread with the butter, leaving a 1-cm/½-inch border. Mix together the sugar and cinnamon, and sprinkle evenly over the butter, then scatter over the raisins.

2 Gently roll up the pastry from one long side. Using a sharp knife, cut through the roll to make 12 even-sized rounds. Place the rounds, flat-side down, on the prepared baking sheets. Use the palm of your hand to flatten out each round slightly. Bake in the preheated oven for 12–15 minutes, or until risen and golden.

3 Transfer the pastries to a wire rack. Put the jam into a small saucepan and heat over a low heat until warm, then strain through a fine sieve into a small bowl to make a smooth glaze. Quickly brush the glaze over the hot pastries. Serve warm or cold.

BAKING & DESSERTS

CHEWY GOLDEN COOKIES

Makes: 30

Prep: 20 mins,
plus cooling & setting

Cook: 12 mins

Ingredients

175 g/6 oz butter or margarine, plus extra for greasing

250 g/9 oz soft light brown sugar

350 g/12 oz golden syrup

3 egg whites

250 g/9 oz rolled oats

280 g/10 oz plain flour

pinch of salt

1 tsp baking powder

2 tbsp icing sugar, to decorate

Method

1 Preheat the oven to 180°C/350°F/Gas Mark 4. Grease several large baking sheets and line with baking paper.

2 In a large mixing bowl, blend the butter, sugar, golden syrup and egg whites together. Gradually add the oats, flour, salt and baking powder, and mix thoroughly.

3 Drop 30 rounded tablespoons of the mixture onto the prepared baking sheets, spaced well apart, and transfer to the preheated oven. Bake for 12 minutes, or until the biscuits are light brown.

4 Transfer to wire racks to cool completely. Mix the icing sugar with a few drops of water to form a thin icing, drizzle over the biscuits and leave to set.

BAKING & DESSERTS

BLUEBERRY SCONES

Makes: 8

Prep: 20 mins, plus cooling

Cook: 20–22 mins

Ingredients

250 g/9 oz plain flour, plus extra for dusting

2 tsp baking powder

¼ tsp salt

85 g/3 oz butter, chilled and diced, plus extra for greasing and to serve

70 g/2½ oz golden caster sugar

115 g/4 oz blueberries

1 egg

100 ml/3½ fl oz buttermilk

1 tbsp milk

1 tbsp demerara sugar

Method

1 Preheat the oven to 200°C/400°F/Gas Mark 6. Lightly grease a large baking sheet.

2 Sift together the flour, baking powder and salt into a large bowl, and stir in the butter. Rub the butter into the flour until the mixture resembles fine breadcrumbs. Stir in the caster sugar and blueberries.

3 Beat together the egg and buttermilk and pour into the bowl. Mix to a soft dough. Turn out the dough onto a floured work surface and knead gently.

4 Shape and gently pat the dough into an 18-cm/7-inch round. Use a sharp knife to cut into eight even-sized wedges. Place the wedges on the prepared baking sheet. Brush the tops of the scones with the milk and sprinkle over the demerara sugar. Bake in the preheated oven for 20–22 minutes, or until risen and golden brown. Transfer to a wire rack to cool, then serve with butter.

BAKING & DESSERTS

APPLE FRITTERS

Serves: 4

Prep: 20 mins,
plus standing

Cook: 20–24 mins

Ingredients

300 g/10½ oz eating apples,
such as Granny Smith,
peeled, cored and cut
into chunks

1 tsp lemon juice

2 eggs, separated

sunflower oil, for deep-frying
and greasing

150 ml/5 fl oz milk

15 g/½ oz butter, melted

70 g/2½ oz plain white flour

70 g/2½ oz plain
wholemeal flour

2 tbsp sugar

¼ tsp salt

Cinnamon glaze

55 g/2 oz icing sugar

½ tsp ground cinnamon

1 tbsp milk, plus extra,
if needed

Method

1 To make the cinnamon glaze, sift the sugar and
cinnamon into a small bowl and make a well
in the centre. Slowly stir in the milk until smooth,
then set aside.

2 Put the apples in a small bowl, add the
lemon juice, toss and set aside. Beat the egg
whites in a separate bowl until stiff peaks form,
then set aside.

3 Heat enough oil for deep-frying in a deep-fat
fryer or large, heavy-based saucepan until it
reaches 180–190°C/350–375°F, or until a cube of
bread browns in 30 seconds.

4 Meanwhile, put the egg yolks and milk into a
large bowl and beat together, then stir in the
butter. Sift in the white flour, wholemeal flour,
sugar and salt, tipping in any bran left in the
sieve, then stir the dry ingredients into the wet
ingredients until just combined. Stir in the apples
and their juices, then fold in the egg whites.

5 Lightly grease a spoon and use it to drop
batter into the hot oil, without overcrowding
the pan. Fry the fritters for 2–3 minutes, turning
once, until golden brown on both sides. Transfer
to kitchen paper to drain, then transfer to a wire
rack to cool. Repeat this process until all the
batter is used.

BAKING & DESSERTS

6 Stir the glaze and add a little extra milk, if necessary, so that it flows freely from the tip of a spoon. Drizzle the glaze over the fritters and leave to stand for 3–5 minutes to firm up. Serve immediately.

★ **Variation**

Replace the eating apples with thick slices of pear in this recipe for a sweeter variation – make sure that the pears aren't over-ripe as they might not hold their shape as well once fried.

STRAWBERRIES & CREAM FILO TARTS

Makes: 4

Prep: 25 mins,
plus cooling

Cook: 8–10 mins

Ingredients

25 g/1 oz butter

85 g/3 oz filo pastry

200 g/7 oz strawberries, plus extra to garnish

2 tbsp strawberry conserve

150 ml/5 fl oz double cream

150 g/5½ oz carton ready-made custard

Method

1 Preheat the oven to 200°C/400°F/Gas Mark 6. Melt the butter in a small saucepan and use some of it to lightly grease four 10-cm/4-inch tartlet tins. Place the tins on a baking sheet. Use scissors to cut the pastry into sixteen 15-cm/6-inch squares.

2 Stack four squares of pastry on top of each other, each at a slight angle. Brush the top and underside of the stack with the melted butter. Press into one of the prepared tins. Repeat with the remaining pastry and butter to make four cases in total. Bake in the preheated oven for 4–5 minutes, or until golden at the edges. Carefully remove from the tins and gently flip over onto the baking sheet. Bake for a further 2–3 minutes, or until golden all over.

3 Transfer the pastry cases to a wire rack and leave to cool for 12–14 minutes. Meanwhile, hull the strawberries and slice into a bowl, reserving eight whole strawberries to garnish. Stir in the conserve. Whip the cream in a bowl until it holds firm peaks, then fold in the custard. Divide the cream mixture between the pastry cases, top with the strawberries and serve garnished with a couple of whole strawberries.

QUICK TIRAMISÙ

Serves: 4

Prep: 15–20 mins,
plus optional chilling

Cook: No cooking

Ingredients

225 g/8 oz mascarpone cheese

1 egg, separated

2 tbsp natural yogurt

2 tbsp caster sugar

2 tbsp dark rum

2 tbsp strong, black coffee, cooled to room temperature

8 sponge fingers

2 tbsp grated plain chocolate

Method

1 Put the mascarpone cheese, egg yolk and yogurt in a large bowl and beat together until smooth.

2 Whisk the egg white in a separate bowl until stiff, but not dry. Add the sugar and gently fold into the mascarpone mixture. Divide half of the mascarpone mixture between four sundae glasses.

3 Place the rum and coffee in a shallow dish and mix together. Dip the sponge fingers into the rum mixture, break into bite-sized pieces and divide between the glasses.

4 Stir any remaining coffee mixture into the remaining mascarpone mixture and divide between the glasses. Sprinkle with the grated chocolate. Serve immediately, or cover and chill until required.

BANOFFEE MERINGUE PIE

Serves: 8

Prep: 15–20 mins,
plus optional cooling

Cook: 12–15 mins

Ingredients

1 x 20-cm/8-inch ready-made all butter round pastry case

400 g/14 oz canned dulce de leche (caramel sauce)

1 large banana

3 large egg whites

175 g/6 oz caster sugar

1 tbsp chocolate shavings

Method

1 Preheat the oven to 190°C/375°F/Gas Mark 5. Place the pastry case on a baking sheet. Spoon the dulce de leche into the case and level the surface with a spatula. Peel and thinly slice the banana and arrange the slices on top of the caramel.

2 Put the egg whites into a clean, grease-free bowl and beat with a hand-held electric mixer until they hold stiff peaks. Gradually mix in the sugar, one spoonful at a time, to make a firm and glossy meringue. Spoon the meringue over the bananas and swirl with the back of a spoon.

3 Bake in the preheated oven for 12–15 minutes, or until the meringue is golden brown. Sprinkle the chocolate shavings over the hot meringue and serve immediately or leave to cool.

BUTTERSCOTCH, MANGO & GINGER SUNDAES

Serves: 4   **Prep: 15–20 mins**   **Cook: 8 mins**

Ingredients

1 large, ripe mango

115 g/4 oz ginger biscuits

1 litre/1¾ pints vanilla ice cream

2 tbsp roughly chopped almonds, toasted

Butterscotch sauce

100 g/3½ oz light muscovado sugar

100 g/3½ oz golden syrup

55 g/2 oz unsalted butter

100 ml/3½ fl oz double cream

½ tsp vanilla extract

Method

1 To make the butterscotch sauce, melt the sugar, golden syrup and butter in a small saucepan and simmer for 3 minutes, stirring, until smooth. Stir in the cream and vanilla extract, then remove from the heat.

2 Peel and stone the mango and cut into 1-cm/½-inch cubes. Place the ginger biscuits in a polythene bag and crush lightly with a rolling pin.

3 Divide half of the mango between four sundae glasses and top each with a scoop of the ice cream. Spoon over a little of the warm butterscotch sauce and sprinkle with the crushed biscuits. Repeat the layers with the remaining ingredients.

4 Sprinkle the almonds evenly over the top of each sundae and serve immediately.

CHOCOLATE PUDDING

Serves: 6　　　　　**Prep: 15 mins**　　　　**Cook: 12–15 mins**

Ingredients

100 g/3½ oz sugar
4 tbsp cocoa powder
2 tbsp cornflour
pinch of salt
350 ml/12 fl oz milk
1 egg, beaten
55 g/2 oz butter
½ tsp vanilla extract
double cream,
to serve

Method

1　Mix together the sugar, cocoa powder, cornflour and salt in a heatproof bowl, and set aside.

2　Pour the milk into a saucepan and heat over a medium heat until just simmering. Do not bring to a boil.

3　Keeping the pan over a medium heat, spoon a little of the simmering milk into the sugar mixture and blend, then stir this mixture into the milk in the pan. Beat in the egg and half the butter, and reduce the heat to low.

4　Simmer for 5–8 minutes, stirring frequently, until the mixture thickens. Remove from the heat and add the vanilla extract and the remaining butter, stirring until the butter melts and is absorbed.

5　Transfer to serving bowls. Drizzle with double cream and serve immediately.

FILO PLUM & ALMOND TART

Serves: 4

Prep: 15 mins, plus cooling

Cook: 21–27 mins

Ingredients

55 g/2 oz butter, softened

4 x 28-cm/11-inch square filo pastry sheets

5 small red plums

1 egg

55 g/2 oz ground almonds

40 g/1½ oz caster sugar, plus 1 tbsp extra for sprinkling

1 tbsp plain flour

custard or cream, to serve (optional)

Method

1 Preheat the oven to 200°C/400°F/Gas Mark 6 and place a baking sheet in the oven to heat up. Melt 15 g/½ oz of the butter in a small saucepan and use some to lightly grease a 20-cm/8-inch round, loose-based tart tin. Brush the filo pastry sheets with the remaining melted butter and layer them in the prepared tin, gently scrunching the pastry around the edge of the tin.

2 Scrunch some foil into a disc and place in the pastry case. Bake in the preheated oven for 4–5 minutes, or until the pastry is just beginning to brown around the edges. Meanwhile, quarter and stone the plums. Put the remaining butter into a bowl with the egg, ground almonds, sugar and flour, and beat together until smooth.

3 Remove the foil and spread the almond mixture in the pastry case. Top with the plum quarters and sprinkle with sugar. Return to the oven and bake for 15–20 minutes, or until the pastry is golden brown and the filling is almost set (it will still be wobbly in the middle). Leave to cool in the tin. Serve warm or cold with custard, if using.

CARAMEL PECAN APPLES

Serves: 4　　　**Prep: 10-15 mins**　　　**Cook: 11-12 mins**

Ingredients

55 g/2 oz unsalted butter

55 g/2 oz light muscovado sugar

4 crisp eating apples, cored and cut into wedges

1 tsp ground cinnamon

4 thick slices of brioche

4 tbsp rum or apple juice

30 g/1 oz pecan nuts

Method

1 Melt the butter in a frying pan and stir in the sugar, apples and cinnamon. Cook over a medium heat, stirring occasionally, for 5–6 minutes, until caramelized and golden.

2 Meanwhile, toast the brioche on both sides until golden.

3 Stir the rum and pecan nuts into the pan and cook for a further minute.

4 Transfer the toasted brioche to warmed serving plates. Spoon the apple mixture over and serve immediately.

PEAR & HAZELNUT PANCAKES

Serves: 4   **Prep: 20 mins**   **Cook: 10 mins**

Ingredients

200 g/7 oz chocolate hazelnut spread

8 ready-made pancakes

4 ripe pears

40 g/1½ oz unsalted butter, melted

2 tbsp demerara sugar

55 g/2 oz toasted chopped hazelnuts, to serve

Method

1 Preheat the grill to high. Warm the chocolate spread gently in a small saucepan until softened.

2 Using a palette knife, spread each pancake with a little of the warmed chocolate spread.

3 Peel, core and chop the pears. Arrange the pears over the chocolate spread, then bring the opposite sides of the pancakes over the filling to enclose it.

4 Lightly brush an ovenproof dish with a little of the melted butter.

5 Arrange the pancakes in the dish. Brush the pancakes with the remaining melted butter and sprinkle with the demerara sugar.

6 Place the dish under the preheated grill and cook for 4–5 minutes, until bubbling and lightly browned.

7 Scatter the toasted hazelnuts over the pancakes and serve hot.

BAKING & DESSERTS

CHOCOLATE BAKED ALASKA

Serves: 6

Prep: 20–25 mins, plus freezing

Cook: 5 mins

Ingredients

500 g/1 lb 2 oz chocolate ice cream

6 ready-made chocolate brownies

2 large egg whites

115 g/4 oz caster sugar

cocoa powder, for dusting

Method

1 Line a 700-ml/1¼-pint pudding basin with clingfilm. Place the ice cream in the basin. Slice off any excess ice cream above the rim of the basin and cut this into smaller chunks. Push the chunks into the gaps around the main block of ice cream. Top with the chocolate brownies, cutting to fit, if necessary, and press down firmly. Place in the freezer for 15 minutes. Preheat the oven to 220°C/425°F/Gas Mark 7.

2 Put the egg whites into a clean, grease-free bowl and whisk with a hand-held electric mixer until they hold firm peaks. Gradually whisk in the sugar, one spoonful at a time, to make a firm and glossy meringue.

3 Remove the basin from the freezer and turn out onto a baking sheet. Quickly spoon and spread the meringue all over the ice cream and the edge of the chocolate brownie base to cover completely. Bake in the preheated oven for 5 minutes, or until the meringue is just set and lightly browned. Serve immediately, lightly dusted with cocoa powder.

MINI APPLE CRUMBLES

Serves: 4   **Prep: 15 mins**   **Cook: 17–18 mins**

Ingredients

2 large Bramley apples, peeled, cored and chopped

3 tbsp maple syrup

juice of ½ lemon

½ tsp ground allspice

55 g/2 oz unsalted butter

100 g/3½ oz porridge oats

40 g/1½ oz light muscovado sugar

Method

1 Preheat the oven to 220°C/425°F/Gas Mark 7. Place a baking sheet in the oven to heat. Put the apples into a saucepan and stir in the maple syrup, lemon juice and allspice.

2 Bring to the boil over a high heat, then reduce the heat to medium, cover the pan and cook for 5 minutes, or until almost tender.

3 Meanwhile, melt the butter in a separate saucepan, then remove from the heat and stir in the oats and sugar.

4 Divide the apples between four individual 200-ml/7-fl oz ovenproof dishes. Sprinkle over the oat mixture. Place on the baking sheet in the preheated oven and bake for 10 minutes, until lightly browned and bubbling. Serve warm

LEMON POSSET

Serves: 4   **Prep: 15–20 mins**   **Cook: No cooking**

Ingredients

grated rind and juice of
1 large lemon

4 tbsp dry white wine

55 g/2 oz caster sugar

300 ml/10 fl oz double
cream

2 egg whites

lemon zest, to decorate

langues de chat biscuits,
to serve

Method

1 Place the lemon rind and juice, wine and sugar
in a bowl. Mix until the sugar has dissolved. Add
the cream and beat with a hand-held electric
mixer until soft peaks form.

2 Whisk the egg whites in a separate bowl, until stiff
but not dry. Gently fold into the cream mixture.

3 Spoon the mixture into four serving glasses.
Decorate with lemon zest and serve immediately
with langues de chat biscuits.

★ **Variation**

This zesty dessert will work well with any citrus
fruit. Try lime or pink grapefruit for fun flavour
variations.

INDEX

INDEX

This edition published by Parragon Books Ltd in 2014
LOVE FOOD is an imprint of Parragon Books Ltd

Parragon Books Ltd
Chartist House
15–17 Trim Street
Bath BA1 1HA, UK
www.parragon.com/lovefood

ISBN 978-1-4723-6348-0
Printed in China

Introduction by Anne Sheasby
Cover photography by Ian Garlick

Notes for the Reader
This book uses both metric and imperial measurements. Follow the
same units of measurement throughout; do not mix metric and imperial.
All spoon measurements are level: teaspoons are assumed to be 5 ml,
and tablespoons are assumed to be 15 ml. Unless otherwise stated, milk
is assumed to be full fat, eggs and individual vegetables are medium,
and pepper is freshly ground black pepper. Unless otherwise stated, all
root vegetables should be peeled prior to using.

Garnishes, decorations and serving suggestions are all optional and
not necessarily included in the recipe ingredients or method. The
times given are an approximate guide only. Preparation times differ
according to the techniques used by different people and the cooking
times may also vary from those given. Optional ingredients, variations or
serving suggestions have not been included in the time calculations.

Vegetarians should be aware that some of the ready-made ingredients
used in the recipes in this book may contain animal products. Always
check the packaging before use.